ENVIRONMENTAL
HAZARDS
OF WAR

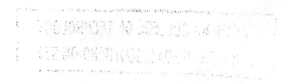

International Peace Research Institute, Oslo
Fuglehauggata 11, N-0260 Oslo 2, Norway
Telephone: 47/2-55 71 50
Cable address: PEACERESEARCH OSLO
Telefax: 47/2-55 84 22

PRIO is an independent international institute of peace and conflict research, founded
in 1959 as one of the first of its kind. It is governed by an international Governing
Board of eight individuals, and it is financed mainly by the Norwegian Ministry
for Culture and Science. All PRIO research is based on open sources and all of
its publications are available to the public.

United Nations Environment Programme
PO Box 30552, Nairobi, Kenya
Telephone: 254/2-33 39 30
Cable address: UNITERRA NAIROBI
Telefax: 254/2-52 07 11

UNEP was established in 1972 by the United Nations General Assembly. It is
governed by an intergovernmental Governing Council consisting of 55 states, elected
from among the member states of the General Assembly. UNEP is the primary
environmental planning and coordinating agency within the United Nations system
and also serves as the focal point for global environmental concerns.

Any findings, opinions, conclusions, or recommendations expressed in this book are
those of the editor and authors and do not necessarily reflect the views of either PRIO
or UNEP.

Military activities and the human environment

*Environmental Hazards of War: Releasing Dangerous Forces in an Industrialized
World* has been prepared at PRIO as a project within the PRIO/UNEP program on
'Military activities and the human environment'. The present volume is an outgrowth
of a select symposium convened by PRIO in cooperation with UNEP in Geneva,
10–14 October 1988, with the local host being UNIDIR.

The book represents the seventh in a UNEP-sponsored series, being the second
under the auspices of PRIO (the first five having been carried out under the auspices
of the Stockholm International Peace Research Institute). The prior six titles (all
edited and co-authored by Arthur H. Westing) were:

Herbicides in War: the Long-term Ecological and Human Consequences (Taylor &
    Francis, London, 210 pp., 1984)
Environmental Warfare: a Technical, Legal and Policy Appraisal (Taylor & Francis
    London, 107 pp., 1984), in cooperation with UNIDIR
Explosive Remnants of War: Mitigating the Environmental Effects (Taylor & Francis,
    London, 141 pp., 1985)
*Global Resources and International Conflict: Environmental Factors in Strategic
    Policy and Action* (Oxford University Press, Oxford, 280 pp., 1986)
Cultural Norms, War and the Environment (Oxford University Press, Oxford, 177
    pp., 1988)
Comprehensive Security for the Baltic: an Environmental Approach (Sage Publica-
    tions, London, 148 pp, 1989).

ENVIRONMENTAL
HAZARDS
OF WAR
Releasing Dangerous Forces
in an Industrialized World

Edited by

ARTHUR H. WESTING

PRIO

International Peace Research Institute, Oslo

UNEP

United Nations Environment Programme

$ SAGE Publications

London • Newbury Park • New Delhi

SAGE Publications Ltd
28 Banner Street
London EC1Y 8QE

SAGE Publications Inc
2111 West Hillcrest Drive
Newbury Park, California 91320

SAGE Publications India Pvt Ltd
32, M-Block Market
Greater Kailash – I
New Delhi 110 048

British Library Cataloguing in Publication data

Environmental hazards of war: releasing dangerous forces in an industrialized
   world. – (PRIO Monographs) (International Peace Research Institute, Oslo)
   1. Ecosystems. Effects of warfare
   I. Westing, Arthur H. II. United Nations, *Environment Programme* III.
   International Peace Research Institute, Oslo IV. Series
   574.5222

ISBN 0-8039-8386-7

Library of Congress catalog card number 90–061319

Typeset by Sage Publications, London
Printed in Great Britain by Billing and Sons Ltd, Worcester

This volume is dedicated to the memory of
Professor Dr Boguslaw Andrzej Molski
(5 January 1932 – 26 March 1989)

Tireless champion of environmental protection,
human justice, and world peace
and
initiator of the
discussions that led to this volume

Contents

Preface

Since the beginning of this century, the world has borne the brunt of a number of truly devastating wars. It is our fervent hope that there will be no repetition of those terrible occurrences. The human and environmental impact of the next war could easily dwarf even those of World Wars I and II for a variety of direct and indirect reasons, even if the use of nuclear or chemical weapons were to be avoided.

This book explores the extent of human and environmental damage that could be expected from a major war in a rapidly industrializing world, with special emphasis on the fast-growing potential for collateral effects via the release of dangerous forces from civil artifacts. It does so in order to reinforce the growing recognition that major war – even without the use of actual weapons of mass destruction – has become an activity in which ends can no longer justify means. We are therefore most pleased to note that the political climate of Europe has been improving dramatically over the past few years, making a future major war in that part of the world, and perhaps elsewhere, ever less likely.

However, given the rapid spread of industrialization throughout the world, with its accompanying storehouse of dangerous forces, nations must fully recognize that hostile actions of any sort could unleash this stored potential for human and environmental devastation.

Both PRIO and UNEP are again pleased to have been able to cooperate in supporting this important project, carried out under the guidance of Dr Arthur H. Westing (Adjunct Professor of Ecology at Hampshire College in Amherst, Massachusetts), the second of a series that explores the various ramifications of peace, environment, and security.

Sverre Lodgaard
Director
PRIO

Mostafa K. Tolba
Executive Director
UNEP

Foreword

The prevention of war, especially of nuclear war, is a task that demands the urgent attention of all. The impact of war on the many-splendored pattern of human existence is inescapable and multi-dimensional. The impact on the environment is particularly important at a time when weapon technology is becoming increasingly sophisticated and increasingly widespread, and the scope for collateral damage ever greater. The issues at stake are not only the unprecedented degree of loss of human life and destruction of property, but also the threat to basic human life-support systems – both economic and environmental – placing the future of all human existence in doubt.

The United Nations Institute for Disarmament Research was therefore glad to be associated with this PRIO/UNEP research project on environmental hazards of war in a rapidly industrializing world. The UNIDIR contribution was modest and, apart from providing facilities for the symposium held in Geneva in October 1988, was pleased to participate in the discussions that took place. UNIDIR association in this project derives from the objective embodied in the UNIDIR Statute that 'The Institute may also develop arrangements for co-operation with other organizations and institutions active in the field of disarmament research...' (Article VI.2). It also complements UNIDIR research on conventional disarmament, which has been the subject of UNIDIR research reports and was the focus of the September 1988 issue of the UNIDIR Newsletter and also the theme of a major UNIDIR conference held in Geneva in January 1989.

Although UNIDIR does not, of course, take a position on the views and conclusions expressed by the editor and authors of this research project, it is convinced that this publication represents an important contribution to the discussion of the subject.

Jayantha Dhanapala
Director
UNIDIR

Glossary of Organizations and Units of Measure

I Glossary of Organizations

CD Conference on Disarmament (Geneva); established (as the Conference of the Ten-Nation Committee on Disarmament) in 1959

IAEA International Atomic Energy Agency (Vienna); established in 1957

ICOLD International Commission on Large Dams (Paris); established in 1928

IUCN International Union for Conservation of Nature and Natural Resources = 'World Conservation Union' (Gland, Switzerland); established in 1948

PRIO International Peace Research Institute Oslo; established in 1959

UNDRO United Nations Disaster Relief Co-ordinator (Geneva); established in 1971

UNEP United Nations Environment Programme (Nairobi); established in 1972

UNESCO United Nations Educational, Scientific and Cultural Organization (Paris); established in 1945

UNIDIR United Nations Institute for Disarmament Research (Geneva); established in 1980

II Units of Measure

The units of measure and prefixes (and the abbreviations) employed in the text are in accordance with the international system (SI) of units (Goldman & Bell, 1981). Standard conversion factors are used (Weast & Astle, 1979-1980, pp. F307-F329).

ampere (A) = unit of electric current (cf. Goldman & Bell [1981, pp. 3–4])

are (a) = 100 square meters = 1 076.39 square feet becquerel
  (Bq) = 1 disintegration per second = $27.027\ 0 \times 10^{-12}$ curie

degree Celsius (°C) = 1 kelvin. To convert temperature in degrees Celsius to temperature in degrees Fahrenheit, multiply by 1.8 and then add 32 exa- (E-) = 10^{18} ×

exabecquerel (EBq) = 10^{18} becquerels = 10^{18} disintegrations per second = 270.270 × 10^6 curies

giga- (G-) = 10^{15} ×

gigawatt (GW) = 10^{15} watts = 10^{15} joules per second

gram (g) = 10^{-3} kilogram = 2.20462 × 10^{-3} pound

hectare (ha) = 10^4 square meters = 0.01 square kilometer = 2.471 05 acres

hect(o)- (h-) = 100 ×

joule (J) = 0.238 846 calorie

kilo- (k-) = 10^3 ×

kilogram (kg) = 2.204 62 pounds

kilometer (km) = 10^3 meters = 0.621 371 statute mile

kilopascal (kPa) = 9.869 23 × 10^{-3} atmosphere = 0.145 038 pound per square inch

kilovolt (kV) = 10^3 watts per ampere

meter (m) = 3.280 84 feet

meter, cubic (m^3) = 10^3 liters = 264.172 US gallons = 219.969 British gallons = 810.713 × 10^{-6} acre-foot

meter, square (m^2) = 10.763 9 square feet

micro- (μ–) = 10^{-6} ×

microsecond (μs) = 10^{-6} second

pascal (Pa) = 9.869 23 × 10^{-6} atmosphere = 145.038 × 10^{-6} pound per square inch

second (s) = unit of time (cf. Goldman & Bell [1981, p. 3])

tonne (t) = 10^3 kilograms = 1.102 31 US (short) tons = 0.984 207 British (long) ton

volt (V) = 1 watt per ampere

watt (W) = 1 joule per second

References

Goldman, D.T., & Bell, R.J. (eds). 1981. *International system of units (SI)*. Washington: US National Bureau of Standards, Special Publication No. 330, 48 pp.

Weast, R.C., & Astle, M.J. (eds). 1979-1980. *CRC handbook of chemistry and physics*. 60th ed. Boca Raton, Florida: CRC Press, [2447] pp.

Introduction

This project, the second major one in the PRIO/UNDP series (and the seventh major one in this overall UNEP program), explores the environmental hazards even of conventional (non-nuclear, non-chemical) war in a rapidly industrializing world. An emphasis is placed on the collateral environmental damage from the release of so-called dangerous forces from nuclear, chemical, and hydrological facilities. The project culminated in legal, political, and related cultural approaches to mitigating the problem.

Much scholarly attention has been devoted to the environmental impact of nuclear war, with the result that the devastating consequences of a second nuclear war are becoming ever more widely accepted and the possibility of its occurrence thereby diminished. Nevertheless, it remains most important not to lose sight of the fact that in may parts of the world conventional war continues to be a routine approach to the resolution of interstate conflict.

Even if a future major war were not to involve the use of nuclear (or chemical) weapons, it could still be environmentally devastating, a fact not widely enough appreciated. It seems clear that even the conventional weapons present today in the arsenals of the major nations could lead to environmental destruction over huge areas for long periods of time. Such devastation becomes increasingly likely as regions become more highly developed and industrialized. This is so because of the release (whether inadvertent of intentional) of radioactive or toxic chemicals or of impounded waters.

The study divides logically into several parts. The *first* part consists of an overview of the likely impact of a major war in an industrializing world (see Chapter 1). The *second* part analyzes both the potential for release, and the environmental impact of, dangerous forces from nuclear facilities (see Chapter 2), chemical facilities (see Chapter 3), and hydrological facilities (see Chapter 4). The *third* part deals with with formal (legal) constraints on the disruption of the environment by war (see Chapter 5) and also with approaches to preventing the release of dangerous forces, and even to eliminating major war itself as a human endeavor (see Chapter 6).

The text of the volume is complemented by a selection of apropos background references (see Appendix 1) as well as basic data on facilities that have the potential for releasing dangerous forces (see

Appendix 2). Excerpts are also provided from relevant international agreements (see Appendix 3) and declarations (see Appendix 4).

The authors of this book (who have been acting in their private capacities) are:

Ms *Margareta Bergström* (Krångede Aktiebolag; S-111 87 Stockholm; Sweden – at the time of this study with the Swedish Ministry of Defence), and authority on systems analysis;

Mr *Jozef Goldblat* (Geneva International Peace Research Institute; CH-1201 Geneva; Switzerland), an authority on international relations, with special emphasis on arms-control law and policy;

Prof. *Allan S. Krass* (School of Natural Science; Hampshire College; Amherst, MA 01002; USA), an authority on theoretical physics as well as on science and public policy;

Prof. Dr. *Jiri Matousek* (Czechoslovak Academy of Sciences; CS-636 00 Brno; Czechoslovakia), an authority on toxicological chemistry as well as on chemical weapons and disarmament; and

Dr *Arthur H. Westing* (International Peace Research Institute Oslo; N-0260 Oslo 2; Norway), an authority on forest ecology as well as on the environmental impact of military activities.

The PRIO/UNEP program is pleased to note that the realization of its goals in this project is greatly facilitated, not only by the insights gained from a select symposium on the same subject previously convened by the Botanical Garden of the Polish Academy of Sciences at Nieborów, 13–17 September 1987, but also by the cooperation of UNIDIR in providing an opportunity for the participants to meet in a setting highly conducive to fruitful interchange.

The authors are pleased to acknowledge valuable advice from Drs Gerard J. Aupers (University of Groningen), Mr Jayantha Dhanapala (UNIDIR), Dr Simon W. Duke (Ohio State University), Prof. Dr Zbigniew Jaworowski (Institute of Nuclear Chemistry & Technology, Warsaw), Mr Sverre Lodgaard (PRIO), Mr Naigzy Gebremedhin (UNEP), Prof Dr Boguslaw A. Molski (Botanical Garden, Warsaw), Dr M. Manfred Schneider (Central Institute for Physics of the Earth, Potsdam), Prof. Dr Nicolai N. Smirnov (Institute of Evolutionary Morphology & Ecology, Moscow), and Prof. Dr Ralf Stöhr (Technical University of Dresden) during the symposium.

The editor is pleased to acknowledge the editorial assistance of Carol E. Westing (Hovseter School, Oslo).

1

Environmental Hazards of War in an Industrializing World

Arthur H. Westing
International Peace Research Institute Oslo

I Introduction

It has become clear to scholars of the subject that a *nuclear* war of even 'modest' proportions would obliterate the artifacts of civilization, would lead to the end of most human life in the theater of military operations, and, indeed, would make most of it uninhabitable into the foreseeable future (Westing, 1987). Fortunately, there is a growing recognition of that danger, and with that recognition a diminishing likelihood of its occurrence (Mueller, 1989).

On the other hand, non-nuclear (and non-chemical) means of war available have now advanced to the point where even resort to *conventional* war could readily obliterate the theater of military operations in an industrialized area. Thus, the purpose of the present chapter is to sketch out – in preparation for the more detailed analyses to follow – the extent to which any major war might disrupt the human environment. The data on release of dangerous forces – whether intended or incidental – are, of course, applicable to any situation, from major war through terrorist actions and sabotage.

The chapter begins by describing some of the effects to be expected from a war on its theater of military operations, first the *direct* impacts and then the *indirect* (collateral) ones. Goldblat provides an analysis of the legal restraints on the impacts of war on the human environment (see Chapter 5; see also Appendices 3 & 4). Some further constraints on the initiation and pursuit of war as it applies to the human environment are examined in the final chapter of the book (see Chapter 6). A broad range of relevant background information is available elsewhere (Westing, 1980; see also Appendix 1).

II The Theater of Military Operations

Many of the nations of the world are becoming ever more highly developed and heavily industrialized. To begin with, the human environment now contains at least 466 civil nuclear-power plants in 26 countries (of which *ca* 429 are currently in operation) (see Appendix 2), plus a number of nuclear-fuel reprocessing plants and nuclear-waste storage sites (Sivard, 1989, pp. 16–17). Secondly, the human environment now contains many tens of thousands of factories, of which – by way of important example – many thousands (employing of the order of nine million workers) manufacture industrial chemicals (see Appendix 2). Indeed, some 72 countries each has at least 1000 chemical workers, of which 13 countries each has fully 100 000 or more. And thirdly, the human environment now contains more than 777 dams, scattered throughout 70 countries, that are at least 15 meters high and impound over 500 million cubic meters of water; in fact, more than 522 of these (in 63 countries) each impounds over 1000 million cubic meters (see Appendix 2), most of them built since World War II.

Destruction of targets in war would be achieved directly by a great variety of instant-action or delayed-action high-explosive and incendiary devices. The extent (area) of destruction could be reasonably circumscribed when the munitions or means of attack employed are discriminate by nature, as some are. On the other hand, some of the munitions themselves (e.g., fuel/air explosives and other blast munitions) and some of the means of munition employment (e.g., massed rocket or bomb attacks) are inherently indiscriminate and would therefore disrupt rather wide areas. Of special interest in the present context is that previous experience (from World War II, from the Korean War of 1950–1953, etc.) has demonstrated unequivocally that *indirect* means of destroying targets can be extraordinarily efficient. For example, the breaching of dams for the purpose of releasing impounded waters has been spectacularly successful. Other dangerous forces that are likely to be released over wide areas in a future war include: radioactive gases or aerosols from nuclear facilities; toxic gases or aerosols from industrial chemical facilities; and, under certain conditions, heat energy from woodlands (via wildfires).

Both the direct and indirect impacts of war on the human environment that have been alluded to above are outlined below in somewhat greater detail.

III Direct Impact

Referred to here is the direct impact of explosive munitions, both fragmentation and blast, and of incendiary munitions. Such an examination serves to indicate the growing extent of their indiscriminate nature and thus of their increasing potential for bringing about incidental (collateral) damage. As is further noted, the increasing level of destructiveness in wartime through the use of these weapons depends not only on their intrinsic nature, but also on how they are employed.

Fragmentation (high-explosive) munitions are an inseparable part of modern warfare (Lumsden, 1978). Such munitions typically depend for their explosive energy on a mixture of 2,4,6-trinitrotoluene (TNT) and powdered aluminum (although several other concoctions are also common); and for their lethality and destructiveness largely on flying metal fragments, and only modestly on blast. High-explosive munitions are stocked in an immense variety of types and sizes and are delivered to their targets by a comparably immense variety of means. Any single high-explosive munition is apt to disrupt the environment to only a modest extent, being lethal and destructive throughout an area of only a relatively few square meters. However, such munitions are fired in staggeringly huge amounts, thereby often disrupting large contiguous areas. During World War II, the total high-explosive munition expenditures came to perhaps 15 million kilograms per day (Westing, 1985). The Second Indochina War of 1961–1975 left a legacy of more than 20 million bomb craters as a semi-permanent feature of the landscape (Westing, 1976, p. 21). Such massive expenditures of munitions in an industrialized region would be certain to release dangerous forces.

Blast munitions have been finding their way into the major arsenals of the world since the time of World War II. They are worth singling out for a moment owing to their individually disruptive nature (Westing, 1976, pp. 51–53,61–62). Blast munitions depend for their effectiveness on the generation of a blast (shock) wave. In one type – the concussion bomb – the blast wave is generated by the explosion of a gelled aqueous slurry of ammonium nitrate and powdered aluminum; in another type – the fuel/air explosive bomb – the blast wave is generated by the explosion of a mixture of air and ethylene oxide (or similarly volatile and combustible compound). In either case, the zone of lethality and destruction from a single blast weapon is likely to encompass an area somewhat larger than one hectare, and thus again provide the potential for collateral damage in an industrialized area.

Incendiary weapons – magnesium-encased thermit (a mixture of powdered aluminum and powdered iron oxide), white phosphorus, napalm, etc. – are extraordinarily useful components of all modern arsenals (Lumsden, 1975). Although the hostile use of fire takes many forms, clearly the most dramatic military application for fire in recent times has been for the decimation of cities. During World War II, the Allied forces aerially attacked several dozen cities with the express intent of destroying them by fire (Hewitt, 1983). Indeed, a number of these attacks have carved out for themselves permanent niches in military history, among them the destruction of Hamburg in October 1943 (Caidin, 1960), of Dresden in February 1945 (Irving, 1963), and of Tokyo in March 1945 (Edoin, 1987). All in all, it is generally recognized that the annihilation of cities is accomplished more expeditiously, less expensively, with higher casualties, and with greater demoralization of the enemy's civilians by incendiary attack than by any other conventional means. A feature of ever increasing prevalence in the incendiary destruction of cities would be the release of highly toxic combustion products. Incendiary attacks for the purpose of creating rural wildfires are touched upon in the next section.

It is important to point out that there has been a discernible tendency in recent decades for warfare to result in ever greater habitat disruption by explosive munitions (Westing, 1980, pp. 2–5). For example, if a comparison is made between munition expenditures by the USA during World War II, in terms of size of theater, with United States munition expenditures during the Korean War and the Second Indochina War, the values are seen to rise from one war to the next. This increasing profligacy in the use of munitions – and thus of expanded environmental disruption – can be illustrated in another interesting way: US munition expenditures per enemy soldier killed during these same three wars also rose from one to the next, in fact, in the startling ratio of 1 to 6 to 18.

The shifting strategy that has been leading to increased violence against nature can perhaps be attributed largely to the growing technical and logistical abilities of an increasing number of nations to devastate large areas on a sustained basis. On the other hand, to a substantial extent warfare has always resulted in a level of environmental damage that is in large part proportional to the aims, the abilities, the will, and the tenacity of the parties to the conflict (Westing, 1984b).

IV Indirect Impact

Referred to here is the indirect damage to the human environment – often of huge proportions – that could be accomplished by attacking (whether intended or otherwise) such targets as nuclear facilities, chemical facilities, hydrological facilities, and combustible woodlands.

Nuclear Facilities
Nuclear power stations, spent nuclear-fuel reprocessing plants, nuclear-waste storage repositories, and other facilities harboring large quantities of radioactive materials are all potential targets in time of war (Cooper, 1978; Ramberg, 1984; see also Chapter 2). As indicated earlier, scattered about in 26 countries of the world can be found over 460 nuclear facilities open to attack (see Appendix 2).

The possibility exists that a destroyed nuclear facility will contaminate a large surrounding area with iodine-131, cesium-137, strontium-90, and other radioactive débris – an area that would be measurable in hundreds or thousands of hectares. The most heavily contaminated inner zone would become life-threatening; an outer zone of lesser contamination would become health-threatening; and a still greater zone beyond would become agriculturally unusable. Such a radioactively polluted area would defy effective decontamination, its degraded status recovering only slowly, over a period of years or decades, as has been demonstrated by the Pacific test islands. The Chernobyl accident of April 1986 suggests very well the disruption to the human environment that could be expected from this direction (Anspaugh *et al.*, 1988; Hippel & Cochran, 1986; Hohenemser, 1988; Rich, 1989; Westing, 1989). Krass points out the important contribution to this and other nuclear accidents of a combination of poor design and human error, including misjudgement and irresponsibility (see Chapter 2). He further stresses the unpredictability of such failures.

Chemical Facilities
Some factories that manufacture industrial chemicals could release explosive or toxic substances into the environment if attacked (Heinisch *et al.*, 1989; see also Chapter 3). Similarly dangerous chemicals in storage or in transit add to this category of threat. Four past events will suggest the range of tragic possibilities:

1 Two ships collided in the harbor of Halifax, Canada in December 1917, one of which contained a cargo of about five million kilograms of explosives (Nash, 1976, pp. 227-228). A fire broke out; and the ensuing explosion killed more than 1600 people, destroyed some 3000 dwellings, and did huge amounts of additional damage.

2 A failure at a liquified natural gas (LNG) storage facility in Mexico City, Mexico in November 1984, led to the explosion and burning of perhaps 10 000 cubic meters of the stored fuel, killing 600 or more people and destroying everything on about 30 hectares (Redman, 1985).

3 An accidental explosion at a chemical (trichlorophenol) factory in Seveso, Italy in July 1976 contaminated a surrounding zone of about 300 hectares with health-threatening levels of 2,3,7,8-tetrachlorodibenzo-*para*-dioxin, necessitating the long-term evacuation of many hundreds of local inhabitants, the sacrificing of thousands of their domestic animals, the destruction of huge quantities of local produce and crops, and the arduous several-year process of decontaminating the affected farmlands, homes, and other local artifacts (Bonaccorsi *et al.*, 1978; Homberger *et al.*, 1979; Westing, 1978).

4 An improper procedure at a chemical (carbaryl insecticide) factory in Bhopal, India in December 1984 led to the escape of a massive cloud of methyl isocyanate, which killed more than 2000 area residents and permanently disabled an even larger number; there was also massive livestock mortality (Bowonder *et al.*, 1985).

The human environment contains many thousands of industrial facilities (and associated bulk carriers), some large number of which could produce similar disasters if attacked (see Appendix 2). Matousek points out that such chemical facilities tend to be concentrated in certain areas, thereby now making disastrous releases almost unavoidable in wartime even if such facilities were not intentional targets (see Chapter 3).

Hydrological Facilities

Dams can provide especially tempting targets (Westing, 1984a, pp. 6–7; see also Chapter 4). Three past events can be outlined by way of example:

1 A spectacular instance can be presented from the Second Sino-Japanese War of 1937–1945 (Harland, 1988; Westing, 1977, p. 54; 1984a, p. 6). In order to curtail the Japanese advance, the Chinese in June 1938 dynamited the Huayuankow dike of the Yellow River (Huang He) near Chengchow. This action resulted in the drowning of several thousand Japanese soldiers and stopped their advance into China along this front. However, in the process the floodwaters also ravaged major portions of Henan, Anhui, and Jiangsu provinces. Several million hectares of farmlands were inundated in the process, and the crops and topsoil destroyed. In terms of direct human impact, the flooding inundated some 11 Chinese cities and more than 4000 villages. At least several hundred thousand Chinese drowned as a result (and possibly many more) and several million were left homeless. Indeed, this act of environmental warfare appears to have been the most devastating single act in all human history, in terms of numbers of lives claimed.

2 During World War II, the Allies in May 1943 destroyed in the same operation two major dams in the Ruhr valley of Germany, the Möhne and the Eder (Brickhill, 1951; Quast, 1949). A vast amount of damage resulted from the breaching of these two containment structures (impounding only 130 million and 200 million cubic meters of water, respectively – and apparently releasing even less: an estimated 120 million and 150 million cubic meters, respectively): (a) 125 factories were destroyed or badly damaged, 25 bridges vanished and 21 more were badly damaged, a number of power stations were destroyed, numerous coal mines were flooded, and various railroad lines were disrupted; (b) some 6500 cattle and pigs were lost, and 3000 hectares of arable land was ruined; and (c) 1300 German lives were lost plus those of unnumbered slave laborers.

3 During the Korean War, US forces pursued a policy of attacking dams in the Democratic People's Republic of [North] Korea (Rees, 1964, pp. 381–382). The destruction of dams was considered by the USA to be among the most successful of its air operations of that war (Futrell *et al.*, 1961, pp. 627–628,637).

As noted earlier, many hundreds of huge impoundments are now scattered throughout the world (see Appendix 2). It is obvious that a substantial proportion of these would make suitable military targets. Indeed, Bergström makes it clear how variously vulnerable to destruction water-impoundment systems are and how devastating the downstream effects can be on the human environment (see Chapter 4).

Combustible Woodlands
Combustible woodlands and the like provide the opportunity for military forces to initiate self-propagating wildfires in enemy territory (Westing, 1984a, pp. 8–9). During the course of its spread, such a fire would release pent-up energy in the woody and other available fuels, destroying or damaging much in its path. As it turns out, there are rather few appropriately combustible rural areas (and these combustible perhaps only at certain times of the year), and thus only limited opportunities for hostile actions of this sort.

Overall, the release of dangerous forces from hydrological, nuclear, or chemical facilities – whether by hostile intent or incidentally – would constitute one of the grave threats to the human environment in any possible major war of the future and, perhaps to a somewhat lesser extent, under any circumstance.

V Conclusion

World War II left its theaters of military operation in shambles: huge numbers of people killed and further huge numbers permanently disabled; scores of cities and industrial areas in ruins; and much farmland and other rural land disrupted. It will be instructive to provide a summary here of the consequences of that war in order to be able to use its parameters as a reference point in visualizing any major future non-nuclear war.

The various countries of the world were, of course, differentially involved in World War II and thus variously affected. To begin with, the 51 million wartime fatalities (of which 65% were civilian) included 18% of the entire Polish population, as well as 11% each of the Yugoslavian and the Soviet populations, 9% of the German population, and 5% of the Austrian population (Westing, 1980, pp. 35–37).[1]

In addition to the many cities and industrial areas that had been left in ruins through the actions of World War II, there also resulted a very high level of agricultural and forestry damage on the former battlefields of that war (Westing, 1980, pp. 51–53). Moreover, three instances of rural devastation in the wartime zones of German occupation are worthy of note: (a) some 200 000 hectares of Dutch farmlands were destroyed by saltwater inundation, representing 17% of all agricultural lands in the Netherlands (Aartsen, 1946); (b) a huge area in far northern

---

[1] As a horrible non-battlefield component of the World War II period, a German attempt to exterminate two ethnic groups led to the death of about 50% of all Gypsies and about 60% of all European Jews (Westing, 1980, pp. 17–18).

Norway – some 1.2 million hectares – was systematically laid waste (Westing, 1980, pp. 123–124); and (c) the forest resources of Poland were systematically pillaged (UNWCC, 1948, p. 496).

The four decades since World War II have witnessed extraordinary advances in technological and industrial capacities in many of the nations of the world. The arsenals of these nations have also been continuously upgraded since World War II, both qualitatively and quantitatively, as have the sustained logistical capabilities of these nations. But far more important, the advances in industrialization have injected into the human environment storehouses of dangerous forces that are likely to be released by future hostilities. Thus, even a future non-nuclear war could readily dwarf World War II in its human and environmental impacts. Moreover, the losses would inevitably include the invaluable cultural heritage of the world that has accumulated and survived over the millennia.

References

Aartsen, J.P.v. 1946. Consequences of the war on agriculture in the Netherlands. *International Review of Agriculture*, Rome, 37:5S–34S,49S–70S,108S–123S.

Anspaugh, L.R., Catlin, R.J., & Goldman, M. 1988. Global impact of the Chernobyl reactor accident. *Science*, Washington, 242:1513–1519.

Bonaccorsi, A., Fanelli, R., & Tognoni, G. 1978. In the wake of Seveso. *Ambio*, Stockholm, 7:234–239.

Bowonder, B., Kasperson, J.X., & Kasperson, R.E. 1985. Avoiding future Bhopals. *Environment*, Washington, 27(7):6–13,31–37.

Brickhill, P. 1951. *Dam busters*. London: Evans Brothers, 269 pp. + 13 plates.

Caidin, M. 1960. *The night Hamburg died*. New York: Ballantine, 158 pp.

Cooper, C.L. 1978. Nuclear hostages. *Foreign Policy*, Washington, 1978(32): 127–135.

Edoin, H. 1987. *The night Tokyo burned*. New York: St Martin's Press, 248 pp. + 8 plates.

Futrell, R.F., Mosely, L.S., & Simpson, A.F. 1961. *United States Air Force in Korea 1950–1953*. New York: Duell, Sloan & Pearce, 774 pp. + plates.

Harland, D. 1988. Once more unto the breach. *New Scientist*, London, 119(1622): 31–32.

Heinisch, E., Kläss, V., & Klein, S. 1989. *Kriegsuntauglichkeit moderner Industriegesellschaften Beispiel Chemieindustrie: das Katastrophenpotential chemischer Industrieanlagen unter Berücksichtigung spezieller geoökologischer und ökotoxikologischer Aspekte [Incompatibility with war of modern industrial corporations, for example, the chemical industry: the potential for catastrophe of chemical industrial installations in consideration of special geo-ecological and eco-toxicological aspects]* (in German). [East] Berlin: DDR-Komitee für wissenschaftliche Fragen der Sicherung des Friedens und der Abrüstung, Informationen No. 2/1989, 55 pp.

Hewitt, K. 1983. Place annihilation: area bombing and the fate of urban places. *Annals of the Association of America Geographers*, Washington, 73:257–284.

Hippel, F.v., & Cochran, T.B. 1986. Chernobyl: the emerging story: estimating long-term health effects. *Bulletin of the Atomic Scientists*, Chicago, 43(7):18–24.

Hohenemser, C. 1988. Accident at Chernobyl: health and environmental consequences and the implications for risk management. *Annual Review of Energy*, Palo Alto, Calif., 13:383–428.

Homberger, E., Reggiani, G., Sambeth, J., & Wipf, H.K. 1979. Seveso accident: its nature, extent and consequences. *Annals of Occupational Hygiene*, Oxford, 22:327–370.

Irving, D. 1963. *Destruction of Dresden*. London: William Kimber, 255 pp.

Lumsden, M. 1975. *Incendiary weapons*. Stockholm: Almqvist & Wiksell, 255 pp. + 12 plates.

Lumsden, M. 1978. *Anti-personnel weapons*. London: Taylor & Francis, 299 pp. + 14 plates.

Mueller, J. 1989. *Retreat from doomsday: the obsolescence of major war*. New York: Basic Books, 327 pp.

Nash, J.R. 1976. *Darkest hours: a narrative encyclopedia of worldwide disasters from ancient times to the present*. Chicago: Nelson-Hall, 812 pp.

Quast, H. 1949. [Destruction and reconstruction of the Möhne and Eder dams] (in German). *Wasser- & Energiewirtschaft* (now *Wasser, Energie, Luft*), Baden, Switz., 41:135–139,149–154.

Ramberg, B. 1984. *Nuclear power plants as weapons for the enemy: an unrecognized military peril*. Berkeley: University of California Press, 193 pp.

Redman, J. 1985. Pemex: the forgotten disaster. *Chemical Engineer*, Rugby, UK, 1985(418):16–17.

Rees, D. 1964. *Korea: the limited war*. New York: St Martin's Press, 511 pp. + 15 plates.

Rich, V. 1989. Chernobyl: Soviet data made public. *Nature*, London, 338:367.

Sivard, R.L. 1989. *World military and social expenditures 1989*. 13th ed. Washington: World Priorities, 60 pp.

UNWCC. 1948. *History of the United Nations War Crimes Commission and the development of the laws of war*. London: His Majesty's Stationery Office, 592 pp.

Westing, A.H. 1976. *Ecological consequences of the Second Indochina War*. Stockholm: Almqvist & Wiksell, 119 pp. + 8 plates.

Westing, A.H. 1977. *Weapons of mass destruction and the environment*. London: Taylor & Francis, 95 pp.

Westing, A.H. 1978. Ecological considerations regarding massive environmental contamination with 2,3,7,8-tetrachlorodibenzo-*para*-dioxin. In: Ramel, C. (ed.). *Chlorinated phenoxy acids and their dioxins: mode of action, health risks and environmental effects*. Stockholm: Swedish Natural Science Research Council, Ecological Bulletin No. 27, 302 pp.: pp. 285–294.

Westing, A.H. 1980. *Warfare in a fragile world: military impact on the human environment*. London: Taylor & Francis, 249 pp.

Westing, A.H. 1984a. Environmental warfare: an overview. In: Westing, A.H. (ed.). *Environmental warfare: a technical, legal and policy appraisal*. London: Taylor & Francis, 107 pp.: pp. 3–12. [a UNEP book]

Westing, A.H. 1984b. How much damage can modern war create? In: Barnaby, F. (ed.). *Future war*. London: Michael Joseph, 192 pp.: pp. 114–124.

Westing, A.H. 1985. Misspent energy: munition expenditures past and future. *Bulletin of Peace Proposals*, Oslo, 16:9–10.

Westing, A.H. 1987. Ecological dimension of nuclear war. *Environmental Conservation*, Geneva, 14:295–306.

Westing, A.H. 1989. Reflections on the occasion of the third anniversary of the Chernobyl disaster. *Environmental Conservation*, Geneva, 16:100–101.

2

The Release in War of Dangerous Forces from Nuclear Facilities

Allan S. Krass

Hampshire College, Amherst, Massachusetts

I Introduction

The nuclear industry has been created in its entirety since World War II, and no military attack against an operating nuclear facility has ever been carried out anywhere in the world. So there is no historical basis for an analysis of the impact of a major war on nuclear facilities. Nevertheless, it is important to call attention to this new risk because of its potentially catastrophic consequences. Most people would rank radioactivity at or near the top of their list of 'dangerous forces', and the amounts of radioactivity stored in the nuclear facilities of the world are enormous beyond imagination. The possible release of huge quantities of radioactive material in another major war adds an entirely new and frightening dimension to the already awesome destruction experienced in the two great wars of this century.

Therefore, however speculative, it is worthwhile to assess the novel risks posed by nuclear facilities in war. This assessment begins with a description of the distribution of nuclear facilities and identifies nuclear power reactors as the principal source of risk. The threat posed by nuclear power facilities is the possible release of large quantities of radioactive material, so that the next step is to identify those isotopes whose quantity, volatility, and biological activity make them especially dangerous to humans and the environment. Then the potential for massive release of these isotopes can be assessed by looking at the record of major peacetime accidents at nuclear power facilities. This record is not rich enough in data to allow confident predictions, but it does at least suggest some areas in which a wartime environment could contribute to an increased risk of major releases. The chapter ends with a discussion of the strategic incentives and deterrents that might encourage or inhibit attacks on nuclear power facilities in wartime, and with a brief discussion of possible actions that might be taken during peacetime in order to reduce the risks to nuclear facilities in wartime.[1]

II Nuclear Facilities: Types and Distributions

Radioactive materials are found in many places in a modern society. They are used in university and other laboratories for research; in industry for a variety of purposes; in hospitals for research, diagnosis, and treatment; and in nuclear-weapon facilities for research, development, and production. And they are present in greater or lesser amounts in every phase of the commercial nuclear-fuel cycle: mining, milling, enrichment, fabrication, power generation, reprocessing, spent-fuel disposal, and – connecting these phases – transportation. Therefore, it is virtually inevitable that releases of radioactive materials would occur to some degree in any war on the territory of many states. However, except for nuclear reactors and reprocessing plants, these releases would be small and would pose no significant or widespread hazard to human health or the environment.

The vast majority of the radioactive material in the world is generated and stored in the commercial nuclear-fuel cycle, primarily in nuclear electrical generating stations. Not only do these contain an intensely radioactive inventory in the reactor core, but most also have spent-fuel pools in which irradiated fuel assemblies are stored awaiting disposal or reprocessing. The next most important concentrations of radioactive materials are found at reprocessing plants, where irradiated nuclear fuel is separated into recyclable materials, such as uranium and plutonium, and high-level wastes, containing mostly fission products (Lipschutz, 1980, Chapter 2). A reprocessing plant contains large amounts of radioactive material, mostly in liquid form; and most of the high-level wastes are stored in tanks near the reprocessing plants (Lipschutz, 1980, pp. 195–201). Although much planning and research has been carried out for the vitrification and deep geological disposal of high-level wastes, no waste has yet been disposed of in this way. If it were to be implemented, this procedure would effectively remove high-level wastes from any danger of release in wartime.

Even in the absence of safe disposal for high-level radioactive wastes, the danger of wartime releases from reprocessing plants and waste storage facilities is considerably less important than that from nuclear power plants. There are only about 20 reprocessing plants in the world, located in less than a dozen countries (Dennis, 1984, p. 353; Sivard, 1989, pp. 16–17). Only two of these are really large facilities, one in France and the other in the United Kingdom. This

---

[1] Not dealt with in this chapter are the effects of nuclear attacks on nuclear facilities (see Fetter & Tsipis, 1981); nor are the risks of sabotage or terrorist attacks (see Goldman & Lobner, 1982; Leventhal & Alexander, 1987).

Table 2.1 *Nuclear Power Reactors in the World: Numbers and Types*

Territory	In operation		Under construction		Shut down
	Total (No.)	Of which PWR (No.)	Total (No.)	Of Which PWR (No.)	
Argentina	2	0	1	0	0
Belgium	7	7	0	–	1
Brazil	1	1	1	1	0
Bulgaria	5	5	2	2	0
Canada	18	0	4	0	3
China	0	–	3	3	0
Cuba	0	–	2	2	0
Czechoslovakia	8	8	8	8	1
Finland	4	2	0	–	0
France	55	49	9	9	5
German DR	5	5	6	6	0
FR Germany	23	13	2	1	6
Hungary	4	4	0	–	0
India	6	0	8	0	0
Iran	0	–	2	2	0
Italy	2	1	0	–	2
Japan	38	17	12	6	1
Korea, Rep	8	7	1	1	0
Mexico	0	–	2	0	0
Netherlands	2	1	0	–	0
Pakistan	1	0	0	–	0
South Africa	2	2	0	–	0
Poland	0	–	2	2	0
Romania	0	–	5	0	0
Spain	10	7	0	–	0
Sweden	12	3	0	–	1
Switzerland	5	3	0	–	0
Taiwan	6	2	0	–	0
United Kingdom	40	0	2	1	3
USA	108	71	7	5	11
USSR	56	25	26	21	3
Yugoslavia	1	1	0	–	0
World	*429*	*234*	*105*	*70*	*37*

Sources and notes: The data are as at 31 December 1988 (IAEA, 1989, Tables 1, 2, & 13). PWR = pressurized light-water-moderated and cooled reactor. Table prepared by A.H. Westing.

must be compared with the 26 countries that currently operate a total of 429 nuclear power reactors (see Table 2.1). In addition, whereas the potential for local environmental and health hazards of release from reprocessing plants and waste storage facilities is severe, the possibility is extremely small of the kind of widespread effects that were seen in the Chernobyl accident (see Section IV below). Nuclear reprocessing plants and waste storage facilities do not operate at the high temperatures that nuclear reactors do, and the potential for steam or hydrogen explosions, or for graphite fires leading to violent breaches of containment, does not exist at these facilities.

An interesting possible exception to the generalization that reprocessing plants or waste storage facilities are relatively safe is an accident at a Soviet waste storage facility, that occurred in September 1957 (Rich, 1989; Trabalka et al., 1980). The USSR has never fully explained what happened, but it is clear from a wide variety of indirect sources that some event resulted in the radioactive contamination of a large area near the city of Kyshtym in the Ural Mountains. One possibility is that a chemical explosion (or possibly even a criticality excursion) took place in buried liquid wastes at a reprocessing plant (Medvedev, 1979). However, the incident has little relevance to the risks at modern waste storage facilities. The disposal methods used at the Kyshtym site were exceptionally primitive, and are no longer in use.

For the above reasons, the risks posed by reprocessing plants and waste storage facilities are not considered further here. Rather, the focus is on the risk of major releases from the cores of nuclear power plants. Although substantial amounts of radioactivity are present in the spent fuel pool, they are not in a form which could lead to catastrophic or widespread release (Mullen, 1987).

It is most important to point out the predominance of light-water reactors throughout the world over all other types (see Table 2.1). Nuclear reactors are characterized by the materials they use to cool the reactor core and to moderate (i.e., slow down to thermal energies) the neutrons that cause nuclear fission. A light-water reactor, such as Three Mile Island Unit 2 in Pennsylvania, USA, at which a major accident occurred in 1979 (see Section IV below), uses ordinary ('light', as opposed to 'heavy') water for both purposes. Of the nuclear reactors in operation, 55% are of this type, and of those under construction, 67% (see Table 2.1). The Chernobyl reactor is a light-water-cooled, graphite-moderated reactor, and only the USSR uses this type. In recent years, the USSR has begun to move toward a greater reliance on light-water reactors. Of the 26 nuclear power plants currently under construction in the USSR, 21 are light-water reactors and only five are light-water-cooled, graphite-moderated reactors (IAEA, 1989, Table 2).

Other types of nuclear reactors use gases or heavy water as coolants or moderators, and there is a small number of liquid-metal fast-breeder reactors that use liquid sodium as coolant and do not employ a moderator. For example, the United Kingdom relies almost entirely on gas-cooled reactors, whereas Romania is building heavy-water-moderated reactors (IAEA, 1989, Tables 1 & 2). The British gas-cooled reactors pose significantly smaller risks of catastrophic releases of radioactivity than light-water reactors and light-water-cooled, graphite-moderated reactors (Spiewak & Weinberg, 1985).

Light-water reactors are the focus of this study because they are much more common than the other types, carry the greatest safety risks (with the possible exception of light-water-cooled, graphite-moderated reactors), and have been by far the most extensively studied. Ironically, the most serious accident, at Chernobyl, occurred in a reactor type (light-water-cooled, graphite-moderated reactor) for which there is probably the least available information on risk assessment (Donahue *et al.*, 1987). This serves to emphasize the tentative nature of the present analysis.

III Radioactive Releases and their Assessment

The essential components of a nuclear reactor are: (a) the core, where the heat and radioactivity are generated; (b) the cooling system, which circulates coolant through the core and removes the heat; (c) the containment system, which in most plants consists of several layers of steel and concrete; and (d) various emergency and safety systems, designed to prevent accidents from damaging the core.

The most dangerous radioactivity in the core consists of fission fragments. These represent a wide variety of intensely radioactive nuclides, many of which are biologically active. The nuclei produced in any particular fission are unpredictable, but the statistical distribution of them over a large number of fissions is well known (Inglis, 1973, p. 109). Therefore, all nuclear reactors contain more or less the same spectrum of fission products, and their quantities are proportional to the power generated by the reactor in normal operation, and by the length of time the fuel has been exposed.

The radioactive half-lives of fission fragments range from small fractions of a second to hundreds of years. When the reactor is first started up, the inventories of all fission products begin to grow, but those with short half-lives quickly reach an equilibrium concentration that is proportional to the isotope's half-life and the reactor power level. Since normal practice is to keep fuel in the reactor for three years (Nero, 1979, p. 37), isotopes with half-lives longer than this do not reach equilibrium, but instead are present in amounts proportional to the total energy the fuel has produced during its time in the reactor.

The radioactive inventory of a nuclear reactor has a very different character from the fallout from a nuclear weapon. The entire generation of energy in a nuclear explosion takes place in less than one microsecond (Glasstone & Dolan, 1977, p. 17), so there is no time for the long-lived isotopes to build up as they do in reactor fuel. Therefore, even though the total amount of radioactivity released by a one 'megaton' nuclear weapon (a weapon that releases *ca* 4×10^{15} joules of energy) is initially hundreds of times greater than that released in the worst imaginable nuclear reactor accident, the reactor

Table 2.2   *Nuclear Power Reactors in the World: Net Electrical Power and Radioactive Inventory*

Territory	In operation (No.)	Net power capacity (GW[e])	Radioactive inventory	
			Iodine (EBq)	Cesium (EBq)
Argentina	2	0.9	2	1
Belgium	7	5.5	15	6
Brazil	1	0.6	2	1
Bulgaria	5	2.6	7	3
Canada	18	12.2	32	13
Czechoslovakia	8	3.3	9	4
Finland	4	2.3	6	2
France	55	52.6	140	56
German DR	5	1.7	5	2
FR Germany	23	21.5	57	23
Hungary	4	1.6	4	2
India	6	1.2	3	1
Italy	2	1.1	3	1
Japan	38	28.3	75	30
Korea, Rep	8	6.3	17	7
Netherlands	2	0.5	1	1
Pakistan	1	0.1	0	0
South Africa	2	1.8	5	2
Spain	10	7.5	20	8
Sweden	12	9.7	26	10
Switzerland	5	3.0	8	3
Taiwan	6	4.9	13	5
United Kingdom	40	11.9	32	13
USA	108	95.3	254	102
USSR	56	33.8	90	36
Yugoslavia	1	0.6	2	1
World	*429*	*310.8*	*828*	*334*

Sources and notes: Number of nuclear power plants in operation and their net electrical power capacity are as at 31 December 1988 (IAEA, 1989, Table 1). GW(e) = 10^9 watts (electrical). Radioactive inventory is for iodine-131 (half-life, 8.07 days) and for cesium-134 (half-life, 2.05 years) plus cesium-137 (half-life, 30.2 years). EBq = 10^{18} becquerels. It assumes continuous plant operation at full capacity, leading to the following rates of generation (Nero, 1979, pp. 36–37): for the iodine, sufficient to disintegrate at the rate of 2.664 x 10^9 becquerels per watt (electrical); and for the cesium, sufficient to disintegrate at the rate of 1.073 x 10^9 becquerels per watt (electrical). Table prepared by A.H. Westing.

contamination persists for a much longer time. One comparison shows that after five years the remaining radioactivity from a nuclear reactor accident would be 100 times greater than that from a one 'megaton' bomb (Fetter & Tsipis, 1981, p. 38).

A number of radioactive isotopes of significance to biological systems is present in the inventory of nuclear power plants (see Table 2.2). Three isotopes of two elements appear to be the most dangerous to humans, because they combine high volatility, a relatively long half-life, and a chemical affinity for biological systems. One is iodine-131 (half-life, 8.07 days), which is highly volatile under certain accident conditions, is taken up by fresh fruits and vegetables and by cows grazing on contaminated grass, and tends to concentrate in the thyroid gland of humans and other mammals, especially of immature ones (Gofman, 1981, pp. 642–657). The other two are cesium-134 (half-life, 2.05 years) and cesium-137 (half-life, 30.2 years) which concentrate in muscle tissue and contaminate meat, but whose transfer to humans through the food chain is less well understood than that of iodine (Gofman, 1981, pp. 540–543). Cesium contamination of reindeer meat in northern Scandinavia has been one of the major economic impacts of the Chernobyl accident (Reisch, 1987).

One other group of isotopes, the noble gases krypton and xenon, tend to have a large fraction of their inventory released in many accident sequences. But they are chemically inert, their radiation is only weakly penetrating, and they diffuse rapidly in the atmosphere, causing their effects to be relatively minor and confined to external doses in the immediate vicinity of the power plant (Cohen, 1987).

In order for large amounts of fission products to be released from a nuclear reactor, the core must be severely damaged and the containment breached or penetrated. The core of a light-water reactor is normally submerged in cooling water; and the loss of this coolant is necessary, but not sufficient, to cause significant core damage (Golay *et al.*, 1988, p. 8). The loss of moderator shuts down the nuclear chain reaction, but the radioactive material in the core will continue to produce substantial amounts of heat. Heat from residual decay in a typical reactor represents about 7% of the thermal power generated just before shutdown. This can amount to 200×10^9 watts (thermal) or more in a large modern reactor (Nero, 1979, p. 54).

Unless the core can be reflooded in a matter of minutes, it will become so hot that the zirconium cladding of the fuel rods can react with water vapor to generate hydrogen, creating the potential for an explosion or fire inside the containment. Oxidation of the fuel cladding can then lead to disintegration of the fuel assemblies and a progressive collapse of the core. Blockages can cut off emergency coolant flow and create hot spots where fuel melting can begin. Further collapse of the molten core creates the possibility of massive steam explosions when molten fuel comes in contact with residual water in the reactor vessel. A molten core can actually melt through the reactor vessel and fall into the outer containment, creating further opportunities for steam explosions, some of which could propel missiles with enough force to breach the outer containment and release large portions of the radioactive inventory to the atmosphere (Coppinger & Krass, 1978).

This is one example of a loss-of-coolant accident, which is generally taken to be the most serious accident against which safety systems must be designed (Golay *et al.*, 1988, p. 8). A loss-of-coolant accident can be created by a variety of initiating events, such as a pipe break (Lewis *et al.*, 1975, pp. S81–S93), or a loss of off-site power, followed by a failure of on-site auxiliary power systems (Golay *et al.*, 1988, p. 11). Light-water reactors employ a number of backup systems, such as the auxiliary feed-water system and emergency core-cooling system, which depend on a reliable supply of electric power to drive pumps and operate valves (Spiewak & Weinberg, 1985, p. 432). In the case of a loss-of-off-site-power accident, the power must be provided by on-site diesel generators, which tend to have relatively high start-up failure rates even in peacetime (Golay *et al.*, 1988, p. 8). If they do not start up, then the only power supplies are direct-current batteries, designed to work only for limited periods. They will fail unless off-site power is restored within two to six hours (Golay *et al.*, 1988, p. 12).

Even the seemingly invulnerable containment structure – which in many light-water reactors surrounds the reactor vessel and primary cooling system with thick barriers of steel and reinforced concrete – cannot be counted on to maintain its integrity in a serious accident. The containment is designed to hold under the conditions postulated for a so-called design-basis accident, which involves the rupture of any one pipe within the containment. Even if the calculations supporting this design criterion are accepted as reliable, there remains the possibility of more severe accidents that could puncture or rupture the containment. The Chernobyl disaster was an example of an accident that exceeded the design basis of the containment (Pollard, 1987).

IV The Lessons of Experience

The assessment of risk of nuclear power facilities has been largely a theoretical exercise. Major nuclear accidents have too low a frequency to permit empirically grounded risk estimates (Whipple & Starr, 1988, p. 21). The model for such assessments is a reactor safety study that was carried out by the United States Nuclear Regulatory Commission (Rasmussen *et al.*, 1975). However, that study was widely criticized for unrealistic assumptions and serious methodological flaws (Hippel, 1977; Hubbard & Minor, 1977; Lewis *et al.*, 1975; Yellin, 1976). It suffered a further loss of credibility four years after its release when the Nuclear Regulatory Commission itself withdrew its endorsement of the reliability of the numerical risk estimates (NRC, 1979, p. 3; Rogovin & Frampton, 1980). Despite this inauspicious beginning, such assessments continue to be done – at least 20 have been carried out for nuclear reactors in the USA (Okrent, 1987, p. 298) – even as critics have continued to challenge their usefulness as guides to policy-making (MacKenzie, 1984).

Some perspective on theoretical estimates of nuclear reactor risks can be gained by looking at the several serious accidents that have occurred to date, a number of which resulted in significant releases of radioactivity to the environment. However, there is a danger in trying to generalize from small data bases, especially for nuclear energy, which has become so highly politicized over the past two decades. There are both ideological and economic axes to grind, so people tend to interpret any new evidence in ways that reinforce their preconceptions. This has been particularly evident in analyses of two of the four accidents summarized below, Three Mile Island and Chernobyl.

Windscale

One of the earliest nuclear accidents occurred at Windscale, United Kingdom, in October 1957 in an air-cooled, graphite-moderated plutonium production reactor (Auxier, 1986). Operators carrying out a procedure that was required to release stored energy in the moderator were misled by false readings on two temperature sensors and believed the reactor to be cooling down too quickly. They restarted the reactor, causing it to overheat locally, and started a uranium-graphite fire that burned for four days before being extinguished by flooding the core with water. During this period radioactive material was released into the environment which was disintegrating at the rate of more than 30×10^{15} becquerels (Powers et al., 1987, p. 10), of which iodine-131 accounted for 700×10^{12} becquerels, cesium-137 for 20×10^{12} becquerels, and strontium-90 (half-life, 28.1 years) plus strontium-91 (half-life, 9.67 hours) for 3×10^{12} becquerels (Auxier, 1986, p. 89). The effects of the release were apparently confined to an area of about 300 000 hectares, but with the only serious effects over an area about one-tenth that size (Auxier, 1986, p. 87). However, it should be noted that the Windscale accident occurred in the early days of nuclear power when techniques of radiation monitoring were primitive and inconsistently employed.

Brown's Ferry

In March 1975, a worker at the Brown's Ferry nuclear power station in Alabama, USA (a boiling light-water-cooled and moderated reactor) was using a candle to test for air leaks in a cable duct (Hubbard & Minor, 1977, pp. 27–38). The flame ignited electrical cable insulation. The fire spread quickly and destroyed 1600 cables, all of which had been routed through the same tunnel. All of the emergency core-cooling systems were disabled, and the plant was for some time highly vulnerable to a meltdown. This accident provides an example of a so-called common-cause failure, in which a single initiating event disables a number of systems that most risk assessments treat as being independent of each other.

One analysis of the Brown's Ferry event concluded that the reactor safety study referred to above (Rasmussen et al., 1975) had underestimated the probability of this event by a factor of 100 (Hubbard

& Minor, 1977, pp. 188–191). Fortunately, the plant operators were able to improvise a cooling system that kept the core covered and that prevented any release of radioactive material from the plant.

Three Mile Island

The accident in March 1979 at the Three Mile Island nuclear power station in Pennsylvania, USA (a pressurized light-water-moderated and cooled reactor) began with a relatively common event, the shutting down of the normal feed-water supply to the steam generators. At this point, the auxiliary feed-water system pumps were turned on, but no water could flow to the steam generators because all of the manual block valves in the auxiliary feed-water lines had inadvertently been left closed after a test procedure a few days earlier (Denning, 1985, p. 35). The reactor safety study referred to above (Rasmussen et al., 1975) had considered the possibility of just such an event and had, in effect, assigned it a probability of zero (Rasmussen et al., 1975, Appendix II, p. 106). It was believed to be 'incredible' that all six block valves would ever be inadvertently closed at the same time.

The Three Mile Island accident proceeded through a series of equipment failures and operator errors to what became a full-scale loss-of-coolant accident (Thomas, 1986). Once the core was uncovered, its temperature quickly exceeded 2000°C, and zirconium-water reactions began. About 50% of the fuel cladding oxidized, generating copious amounts of hydrogen, 320 kilograms of which ignited about ten hours after the onset of the accident (Denning, 1985, pp. 41,50). The hydrogen did not detonate, but 'deflagrated', a slower form of combustion (Alvares, 1986, p. 60). Still, an over-pressure of nearly 200 kilopascals was produced (Denning, 1985, p. 50), large enough to have breached some existing containments (Beyea & Hippel, 1982, p. 53). Extensive fuel melting ensued and a significant portion of the core collapsed into rubble, leaving a large void in the upper center of the core (Eidam, 1986, p. 92). Finally, after nearly 16 hours, cooling was restored to the core, averting a full-scale meltdown (Denning, 1985, p. 41).

Radioactive releases to the environment were remarkably low (Rogovin & Frampton, 1980, Volume II, p. 342). The most important release was of iodine-131 over a period of 41 days, estimated to have been disintegrating at the rate of only about 600×10^9 becquerels (Rogovin & Frampton, 1980, Volume II, pp. 356–357), a much smaller release than had been predicated for an accident of that severity. Apparently most of the iodine at Three Mile Island remained dissolved in the water and was not volatilized, suggesting that if containment integrity can be maintained for several hours or days, then fission product releases may be substantially reduced (Kelber, 1986, p. 50).

Both encouragement and alarm can be drawn from the Three Mile

Island accident. On the positive side were the ability to reestablish cooling of the core after substantial melting had taken place, the ability of the containment to survive a strong hydrogen deflagration, and the surprisingly low releases of radioactivity. On the negative side were the design, maintenance, training, and management deficiencies that led to the initiation of the accident, and the several equipment failures and operator errors during its progress. Three Mile Island can therefore be seen either as a vindication of the defense-in-depth philosophy of the nuclear industry in the USA, or as a lucky hair-breadth escape from catastrophe. There seems to be no objective means of deciding which view is the more valid one.

Chernobyl

No ambiguity applies to the accident of April 1986 at the nuclear power station at Chernobyl, USSR (a light-water-cooled, graphite-moderated reactor): it qualifies as a disaster by any reasonable measure. The accident began as a safety experiment in which the operators attempted to determine if the coasting-down turbine generator could supply emergency on-site power to drive the emergency core-cooling system after a loss of off-site power. However, a series of operator errors, violations of standard operating procedures, and transgressions of the test procedures themselves led to the catastrophe (Kress et al., 1987, pp. 3–4). The result was an exponential increase in the reactor power level – in effect, a slow nuclear explosion. This triggered a steam explosion that was powerful enough to destroy the reactor, breach the containment, and disperse radioactive material into the atmosphere to a height of 1500 meters. Steam-graphite reactions and/or hydrogen and carbon monoxide burning ignited the graphite, leading to the fire that for several days dispersed even more radioactive material from the reactor (Kress et al., 1987, p. 6; Powers et al., 1987, p. 12).

The total radioactive release from the Chernobyl reactor was enormous: virtually all of the noble gases; at least 20% of the iodine, and 10% to 20% of the cesium. The total release was estimated to have been disintegrating at the rate of perhaps 4×10^{18} becquerels. Radioactivity was widely dispersed. Nearly 2% of the cesium inventory was deposited in Sweden alone (Powers et al., 1987, pp. 11,13). Some 31 people, all plant workers or fire-fighters, died as a result of the explosions or of radiation exposure.

The long-term impact of the Chernobyl accident cannot be estimated with any degree of confidence. Not enough is known about the effects of low radiation exposures to allow quantitative predictions of future illnesses or fatalities from radiation-induced cancers or genetic defects. However, it has been necessary for purposes of nuclear policy-making to develop a methodology for estimating radiation effects. The generally accepted, conservative method is based on the hypothesis that health effects can be extrapolated linearly from large doses, where the effects are measurable, to very small doses, where they are not (Lean, 1985, p. 55).

Based on a linear extrapolation, the average added risk of radiation-induced fatal cancers for humans (of all ages and both sexes) is usually taken to be 20×10^{-6} for an effective dose-equivalent corresponding to one year of natural background radiation (UNSCEAR, 1982, p. 11). If it is assumed that as a result of the Chernobyl accident the full population of Europe will receive an average added exposure of the order of 0.7% of natural background radiation over the next 50 years, then the accumulated dose would be about 35% of background in terms of a single year. This would produce an added risk of fatal cancers of 7×10^{-6} per person; when this value is applied to the population of Europe – 700×10^6 – a prediction for Europe of 4900 extra cancer deaths is obtained. To this prediction must be added the extra deaths that would occur outside of Europe, where a larger population will be exposed to smaller doses. Such a calculation is roughly consistent with other estimates of long-term Chernobyl fatalities, for example, 9000 (Cohen, 1987, pp. 1081–1082) and 17 000 (Anspaugh *et al.*, 1988, p. 1517).

The actual number of added long-term fatalities from the Chernobyl accident, if any, will never be known. The predicted added cancer fatalities is far too small a fraction of the normal incidence of cancer fatalities to be measurable. Still, it is prudent to make a conservative estimate of these potential effects rather than to ignore them because they cannot be measured. To ignore them is, in effect, to set them equal to zero, and this can be as misleading as exaggerating them. Therefore, for the purpose of estimating the potential consequences of attacks on nuclear power plants (see Section IV above), the long-term fatalities caused by the Chernobyl accident should be assumed to lie between 1000 and 20 000.

As with Three Mile Island, the lessons of Chernobyl for nuclear risk assessment are mixed. Human error and irresponsibility are even more prominent in this case than at Three Mile Island, but poor reactor design also played an important role in the Chernobyl case. However, advocates of nuclear energy take some encouragement from the absence of prompt off-site fatalities. Risk assessments in the USA have predicted substantial numbers of prompt fatalities with such large and rapid releases of radioactivity, especially when evacuation is delayed, as it was at Chernobyl. Based on the approximately 31 fatalities actually incurred at Chernobyl, and allowing for the possibility of other prompt fatalities in the nearby population under different and possibly more chaotic circumstances, the value 100 is used here as an order-of-magnitude estimate of the prompt fatalities to be expected in a 'typical' major release.

As noted at the beginning of this section, it is not possible to draw reliable generalizations from such a small data base. All that can be said from the four incidents considered here – Windscale, Brown's Ferry, Three Mile Island, Chernobyl – is that real accident sequences are neither readily predictable nor well understood. At the same time, it is clear that real accidents can be considerably less severe than the worst-case scenarios often used by critics of nuclear energy. In particular, loss of critical safety systems need not result in core damage, severe core damage need not result in major radioactive releases, and major radioactive releases need not result in large numbers of casualties. On the other hand, each of these surprises can be explained by factors that may not be operative in other accidents. It is easy to imagine circumstances under which each one of the described accidents could have had far more serious consequences than it did.

The unique public attitudes toward radioactive contamination must be taken into account. This means that even if the effects of an accident are relatively minor in strictly medical or environmental terms, they can still have powerful psychological effects on large numbers of people. Indeed, the most serious health effects of the Three Mile Island accident were judged to be the fear and anxiety experienced by the population near the reactor (Kemeny et al., 1979, p. 13). However, it is likely that during wartime there would be other more immediate and tangible reasons to experience fear and anxiety.

V The Added Risks of a Major War

It goes without saying that catastrophic releases of radioactivity from nuclear power plants could be induced by an attacker determined to do so. Modern conventional bombs, shells, and missiles have the ability to pierce the thickest containment. For example, an 800 kilogram shaped charge can penetrate ten meters of concrete (Builder, 1985, p. 11). But it is not necessary to penetrate the containment directly to cause a catastrophic release. Loss of coolant could be induced in many ways by attacks on the turbine building or control room, neither of which is as protected as the reactor vessel. For example, in one study it was determined that nuclear reactors in the USA would be extraordinarily vulnerable to an attack by a truck loaded with high explosives, even if the truck were detonated off-site (Hirsch, 1987, p. 210). A large 'truck bomb', such as the type used to attack the United States Marine Corps barracks in Lebanon in 1983, can have an effective yield of 5000 kilograms of trinitrotoluene (TNT) (Woodward, 1987, p. 286). Bombs with similar yields can be carried by aircraft and could be used to attack nuclear reactors.

However, even without intentional attacks, there are added risks from accidents or secondary consequences of other military activities. The dominant contributions to the risk of catastrophic failure of nuclear reactors in peacetime are the loss of off-site power, with subsequent failure of auxiliary on-site power, and pipe breaks resulting in loss-of-coolant accidents (Spiewak & Weinberg, 1985, pp. 436,441). To these must be added the empirical evidence of common-mode failure caused by fire (Brown's Ferry) and the major role played by human error in both initiating and exacerbating accident sequences (Windscale, Brown's Ferry, Three Mile Island, Chernobyl). Although typical risk assessments never consider the impact of a war on these risk factors (Spiewak & Weinberg, 1985, p. 445), common sense suggests that all of them would be increased if nuclear power facilities were exposed to a major war, even if it were to remain conventional.

Modern industrial societies are highly dependent on electric power and have tended to rely more and more heavily on centralized power generation and long-distance transmission (Clark *et al.*, 1980, p. 10; see also Chapter 4). Because such grids are both vital and vulnerable they have become high priority targets for attack by adversaries (Clark *et al.*, 1980, p. 27). Such attacks will certainly increase the risk of loss of off-site power to nuclear facilities, as well as the chance that power outages would be of relatively long duration, long enough to exceed the design capacity of on-site systems. These on-site systems, especially the diesel generators, can themselves be damaged or degraded, either as a result of collateral damage from artillery barrages or bombing raids or from shortages of fuel, spare parts, or qualified maintenance personnel.

Detonations of high explosives, either on-site or nearby, can cause pipe breaks, especially in the pipes that emerge from the containment and carry steam to the turbine. Safety systems are designed to be able to cope with a single such pipe break, but a multiple break caused by a bomb or missile could exceed their capacity. Such detonations can also cause fires, either directly or by inducing short circuits in cable ducts or the control room. The control room relies on hundreds of instruments, sensors, and control devices, all monitored and operated by electric power supplied by circuits that could be damaged by nearby detonations.

The potential for human error and misjudgement is also likely to be enhanced in a combat zone. Nuclear reactor operators and technicians would be under increased pressure, could suffer loss of sleep and nevertheless be forced to work extra hours, would be worried about their families, and could be tempted to leave their posts. Of course, there have been occasions when people have behaved exceptionally well under pressure. The Brown's Ferry reactor was eventually saved by imaginative human intervention (Lewis *et al.*, 1978, p. 26), and many operators and fire-fighters behaved with intelligence and courage in the Chernobyl accident, some sacrificing their lives to help bring the fire under control.

Human behavior under stress is inherently unpredictable, which is why human error is so difficult to include in probabilistic risk assessments. Indeed, if it is believed that much of the human error and negligence observed in peacetime nuclear reactor accidents is the result of complacency and boredom, one might even expect the greater alertness and sense of urgency induced by war to improve operator performance. However, it seems more likely that the stressful and frightening atmosphere of a combat zone, especially if it persisted for an extended period, would do more to degrade the reliability of nuclear reactor operators than to improve it.

All of the wartime considerations discussed above apply to the probability portion of the risk assessment, but the effect of war on the *consequences* of an accident must also be examined. In the accidents that have taken place in peacetime, authorities have been able to respond with the full resources of their society, including medical, technical, police, fire, and logistical personnel. Evacuations have been conducted, food supplies have been screened and condemned where necessary, medical care has been made available, looting has been prevented, and so forth. For example, in the Windscale accident, the surrounding community was warned efficiently and environmental survey teams were organized and dispatched promptly (Auxier, 1986, p. 82). But this was in peacetime. The breakdown of all kinds of public services and societal discipline are well known in war, and such breakdown could only exacerbate the consequences of a nuclear accident.

The above analysis leads to the unsurprising conclusion that the risk of catastrophic failure of nuclear reactors is almost certainly increased in war. However, the increase in risk as a result of war cannot be quantified, any more than the normal peacetime risk can be quantified.

VI Strategic and Tactical Considerations

Even though the conventional weapons now available are the most destructive in history, and although much has been made of the high accuracies achievable with new technologies, the intensity and urgency of attacks in war guarantee that discrimination among targets would be difficult and unreliable (see Chapter 1). It is also possible that some nuclear facilities are close to important military targets and therefore highly likely to sustain collateral damage or lose off-site power for extended periods.

There remains the question of intentional attacks on nuclear reactors, either as an attempt to reduce electrical capacity or to terrorize the population. As has already been noted, attacks on energy facilities have been seen as an increasingly attractive tactic in modern wars, and some analysts have extrapolated this tendency to infer a serious threat of attacks on nuclear facilities (Ramberg, 1980). The concern is reinforced by the historical record of attacks on nuclear reactors by Iran and Israel against Iraq, and against South African nuclear reactors by guerrillas, as well as a number of threats or rumors of threats of such attacks (Ramberg, 1980, pp. xv–xx).

However, a concern over intentional attacks on nuclear reactors must be tempered by the recognition than even when such attacks have been carried out in the past, no risk of radioactive release was incurred. All attacks so far have been against reactors which had not yet had their fuel loaded. In the most serious such attack – the Israeli destruction of the Osiraq research reactor in June 1981 – Israel explicitly attributed the timing of the attack to a desire to avoid radioactive releases that would endanger the population of Baghdad (Ramberg, 1980, p. xix). It is debatable whether the destruction of such a small reactor (40 x 10^9 watts [thermal]) would have had serious health effects even if it were operational, but given the intense aversion to radioactive releases among the public, the moral condemnation of Israel would certainly have been even greater than it was if they had waited until a risk of such a release existed.

The essential difference between nuclear power plants and all other energy facilities is radioactivity, and all evidence indicates that people have an especially intense aversion to this property (Crane *et al.*, 1984, pp. 211–247). It is likely that the risk of release of radioactive material would act as a significant deterrent on a potential attacker, especially in a war between neighboring states. One of the major lessons of Chernobyl has been that a reactor meltdown in the Ukraine can cause death and economic hardship from Scandinavia to Greece, and from Italy to Kazakhstan (ApSimon *et al.*, 1988; Morrey *et al.*, 1987). A terrorist act against one state then becomes a terrorist act against many states, perhaps including the attacking state itself.

It is true that nuclear power facilities are an important part of the industrial infrastructure of many states, and also true that this infrastructure has become an increasingly attractive target in modern warfare. But it does not follow that attacks on nuclear facilities will be seen as sufficiently militarily attractive to overcome these deterring factors. The military benefits to be gained from destroying units of nuclear generating capacity would generally be small. Any presumed benefit of such attacks would have to be balanced against the strong condemnation to be expected from world opinion, and even against the risk of the attacking state contaminating its own territory.

Intentional attacks on nuclear facilities during a war can obviously not be ruled out. Indeed, there is some contradiction between the notion that the consequences of radioactive releases is likely to add only marginally to the overall impact of a war, and the argument that attacks on reactors would be inhibited by the fear of the consequences of such releases. The contradiction is partially resolved in recognizing that the psychological aversion to radioactivity creates a deterrent disproportionate to the expected actual consequences. However, such attitudes are notoriously changeable, and there can be no guarantee that inhibitions that are powerful in peacetime will remain so in wartime. Unfortunately, history offers too much contrary evidence to allow for complacency in this regard.

VII Conclusion

Although it is clear that the threat posed by nuclear facilities in wartime is qualitatively unprecedented, it is not clear how serious that threat is in quantitative terms or what technical measures could be taken to ameliorate it. Intentional attacks on nuclear reactors, the purpose of which is to release large quantities of radioactivity, cannot be ruled out. However, they appear to be less likely than the accidental destruction of reactors as a side effect of combat. The Chernobyl accident has shown that reactors can suffer catastrophic failure when damaged or tampered with, but the Brown's Ferry and Three Mile Island accidents have shown that even very serious failures need not result in major radioactive releases. Even if such releases were to take place, it is not possible to estimate with any precision the human and environmental consequences. Indeed, all that can be said with confidence is that however tragic such effects might be in terms of absolute numbers, they will almost certainly be too small to measure except under very special circumstances.

Despite the uncertainties just suggested, it makes sense for countries with nuclear power stations to think about the added risks of a possible war and to have contingency plans ready. For example, Sweden has devised a plan under which reactors threatened with imminent attack would be run at lower power levels to reduce their radioactive inventory and then shut down (Johansson, 1982, p. 24). It makes further sense to keep nuclear power stations well separated from military facilities that might become targets in wartime. However, beyond such straightforward contingency planning, there seem to be few measures that can be taken at reasonable cost to protect reactors from damage in war.

The most obvious and attractive strategy to minimize wartime damage to nuclear reactors would be to reduce the risk of war itself (see Chapter 6). This should include major reductions in military forces, a shift to inherently defensive military postures, and the relaxation of political tensions.

A second strategy to minimize wartime damage to nuclear reactors would be to make them safer in normal operation. This suggests that research and development be actively pursued on a new generation of reactors possessing so-called inherently safe designs (Crane et al., 1984, pp. 83–100; Spiewak & Weinberg, 1985). These would be much less susceptible to both loss-of-coolant and loss-of-off-site-power accidents and could not melt down. Such a transition could justifiably reduce public anxiety over nuclear energy in both peace and war.

References

Alvares, N.J. 1986. Assessment of thermal damage to polymeric materials by hydrogen deflagration in the reactor building. In: Toth, L.M. (ed.). *Three Mile Island accident: diagnosis and prognosis*. Washington: American Chemical Society, 301 pp.: pp. 60–86.

Anspaugh, L.R., Catlin, R.J., & Goldman, M. 1988. Global impact of the Chernobyl reactor accident. *Science*, Washington, 242:1513–1519.

ApSimon, H.M., Gudiksen, P., Khitrov, L., Rhode, H., & Yoshikawa. T. 1988. Lessons from Chernobyl: modeling the dispersal and deposition of radionuclides. *Environment*, Washington, 30(5):17–20.

Auxier, J.A. 1986. Windscale fire. In: Doege, T.C., Wheater, R.H., & Hendee, W.R. (eds). *Proceedings of the international conference on non-military radiation emergencies*. Washington: Pan American Health Organization, 325 pp.: pp. 80–90.

Beyea, J., & Hippel, F.v. 1982. Containment of a reactor meltdown. *Bulletin of the Atomic Scientists*, Chicago, 38(7).52–59.

Builder, C.H. 1985. *Prospects and implications of non-nuclear means for strategic conflict*. London: International Institute for Strategic Studies, Adelphi Paper No. 200, 35 pp.

Clark, W., *et al.* 1980. *Dispersed, decentralized and renewable energy sources: alternatives to national vulnerability and war*. Washington: US Federal Emergency Management Agency, Report No. 2314–F, 326 pp.

Cohen, B.L. 1987. Nuclear reactor accident at Chernobyl, USSR. *American Journal of Physics*, New York, 55:1076–1083.

Coppinger, L., & Krass, A. 1978. *Meltdown at Montague*. Amherst, Mass.: Hampshire College, 66 pp.

Crane, A.T., *et al.* 1984. *Nuclear power in an age of uncertainty*. Washington: US Office of Technology Assessment, Report No. OTA-E-216, 293 pp.

Denning, R.S. 1985. Three Mile Island Unit 2 core: a post-mortem examination. *Annual Review of Energy*, Palo Alto, Calif., 10:35–52.

Dennis, J. (ed.). 1984. *Nuclear almanac*. Reading, Mass.: Addison-Wesley, 546 pp.

Donahue, M., Gardner, R., & Vine, G. 1987. Assessment of the Chernobyl-4 accident localization system. *Nuclear Safety*, Oak Ridge, Tenn., 28(3):297–311.

Eidam, G.R. 1986. Core damage. In: Toth, L.M. (ed.). *Three Mile Island accident: diagnosis and prognosis*. Washington: American Chemical Society, 301 pp.: pp. 87–107.

Fetter, S.A., & Tsipis, K. 1981. Catastrophic releases of radioactivity. *Scientific American*, New York, 244(4):33–39,146.

Glasstone, S., & Dolan, P.J. 1977. *Effects of nuclear weapons*. 3rd ed. Washington: US Departments of Defense & Energy, 653 pp. + slide rule.

Gofman, J.W. 1981. *Radiation and human health*. San Francisco: Sierra Club Books, 908 pp.

Golay, M.W., Manno, V.P., & Vlahoplus, C., Jr. 1988. Nonprescriptive nuclear safety regulation: the example of loss of offsite power. *Nuclear Safety*, Oak Ridge, Tenn., 29(1):6–20.

Goldman, L.A., & Lobner, P.R. 1982. *Review of selected methods for protecting against sabotage by an insider*. Washington: US Nuclear Regulatory Commission, Report No. NUREG/CR-2643, 96 pp. + 7 apps.

Hippel, F.v. 1977. Looking back on the Rasmussen report. *Bulletin of the Atomic Scientists*, Chicago, 33(2):42–47.

Hirsch, D. 1987. Truck bomb and insider threats to nuclear facilities. In: Leventhal, P., & Alexander, Y. (eds). *Preventing nuclear terrorism*. Lexington, Mass.: Lexington Books, 472 pp.: pp. 207–222.

Hubbard, R.B., & Minor, G.C. (eds). 1977. *Risks of nuclear power reactors: a review of the NRC reactor safety study WASH-1400 (NUREG-75/014)*. Cambridge, Mass.: Union of Concerned Scientists, 210 pp.

IAEA. 1989. *Nuclear power reactors in the world*. 9th ed. Vienna: International Atomic Energy Agency, Reference Data Series No. 2, 60 pp.

Inglis, D.R. 1973. *Nuclear energy: its physics and its social challenge*. Reading, Mass.: Addison-Wesley, 395 pp.

Johansson, L. 1982. *Kärnkraft i krig [Nuclear power in war]* (in Swedish). Stockholm: Centralförbundet Folk och Försvar, Försvar i Nutid No. 6, 32 pp.

Kelber, C. 1986. Radiological source term of nuclear power reactors. *Nuclear Safety*, Oak Ridge, Tenn., 27(1):36–57.

Kemeny, J.G., *et al.* 1979. *Need for change: the legacy of TMI*. Washington: White House, President's Commission on the Accident at Three Mile Island, 179 pp.

Kress, T.S., Jankowski, M.W., Joosten, J.K., & Powers, D.A. 1987. Chernobyl accident sequence. *Nuclear Safety*, Oak Ridge, Tenn., 28(1):1–9.

Lean, G. (ed.). 1985. *Radiation: doses, effects, risks*. Nairobi: UN Environment Programme, 64 pp.

Leventhal, P., & Alexander, Y. (eds). 1987. *Preventing nuclear terrorism*. Lexington, Mass.: Lexington Books, 472 pp.

Lewis, H.W., *et al.* 1975. Report to the American Physical Society by the study group on light-water reactor safety. *Reviews of Modern Physics*, New York, 47(supple. 1):1–123.

Lewis, H.W., *et al.* 1978. *Risk assessment review group report to the U.S. Nuclear Regulatory Commission*. Washington: US Nuclear Regulatory Commission, Report No. NUREG/CR-0400, 66 pp.

Lipschutz, R.D. 1980. *Radioactive waste: politics, technology and risk*. Cambridge, Mass.: Ballinger, 247 pp.

MacKenzie, J.J. 1984. Finessing the risks of nuclear power. *Technology Review*, Cambridge, Mass., 87(2):34–39.

Medvedev, Z.A. 1979. *Nuclear disaster in the Urals*. New York: W.W. Norton, 214 pp.

Morrey, M., Brown, J., Williams, J.A., Crick, M.J., Simmonds, J.R., & Hill, M.D. 1987. *Preliminary assessment of the radiological impact of the Chernobyl reactor accident on the population of the European Community*. Luxembourg: Commission of the European Communities, Health & Safety Directorate, 44 pp.

Mullen, R.K. 1987. Nuclear violence. In: Leventhal, P., & Alexander, Y. (eds). *Preventing nuclear terrorism*. Lexington, Mass.: Lexington Books, 472 pp.: pp. 231–247.

Nero, A.V., Jr. 1979. *Guidebook to nuclear reactors*. Berkeley: University of California Press, 289 pp.

NRC. 1979. *NRC statement on risk assessment and the reactor safety study report (WASH-1400) in light of the risk assessment review group report*. Washington: US Nuclear Regulatory Commission, Press Release (18 Jan 79), 6 pp.

Okrent, D. 1987. Safety goals of the U.S. Nuclear Regulatory Commission. *Science*, Washington, 236:296–300.

Pollard, R. 1987. *Nuclear reactor containments: sieve or shield?* Cambridge, Mass.: Union of Concerned Scientists, Briefing Paper, 6 pp.

Powers, D.A. Kress, T.S., & Jankowski, M.W. 1987. Chernobyl source term. *Nuclear Safety*, Oak Ridge, Tenn., 28(1):10–28.

Ramberg, B. 1980. *Nuclear power plants as weapons for the enemy: an unrecognized military peril*. Berkeley: University of California Press, 193 pp.

Rasmussen, N.C., *et al.* 1975. *Reactor safety study: an assessment of accident risks in U.S. commercial nuclear power plants.* Washington: US Nuclear Regulatory Commission, Report No. WASH-1400 (NUREG-75/014), 9 volumes.

Reisch, F. 1987. Chernobyl accident: its impact on Sweden. *Nuclear Safety,* Oak Ridge, Tenn., 28(1):29–36.

Rich, V. 1989. Soviet accidents: thirty-year secret revealed. *Nature,* London, 339:572.

Rogovin, M., & Frampton, G.T., Jr (eds). 1980. *Three Mile Island: a report to the commissioners and to the public.* Washington: US Nuclear Regulatory Commission, Special Inquiry Group, Report No. NUREG/CR-1250, 2 volumes (183+1272 pp.).

Sivard, R.L. 1989. *World military and social expenditures 1989.* 13th ed. Washington: World Priorities, 60 pp.

Spiewak, I., & Weinberg, A.M. 1985. Inherently safe reactors. *Annual Review of Energy,* Palo Alto, Calif., 10:431–462.

Thomas, G.R. 1986. Description of the accident. In: Toth, L.M. (ed.). *Three Mile Island accident: diagnosis and prognosis.* Washington: American Chemical Society, 301 pp.: pp. 2–25.

Trabalka, J.R., Eyman, L.D., & Auerbach, S.I. 1980. Analysis of the 1957–1958 Soviet nuclear accident. *Science,* Washington, 209:345–353. Cf. ibid. 245:806. 1989.

UNSCEAR. 1982. *Ionizing radiation: sources and biological effects.* New York: UN Scientific Committee on the Effects of Atomic Radiation, 773 pp.

Whipple, C., & Starr, C. 1988. Nuclear power safety goals in light of the Chernobyl accident. *Nuclear Safety,* Oak Ridge, Tenn., 29(1):20–28.

Woodward, B. 1987. *Veil: the secret wars of the CIA 1981–1987.* New York: Simon & Schuster, 543 pp. + 16 plates.

Yellin, J. 1976. Nuclear Regulatory Commission's reactor safety study. *Bell Journal of Economics,* Hicksville, NY, 7(1):317–339.

3

The Release in War of Dangerous Forces from Chemical Facilities[1]

Jiri Matousek
Czechoslovak Academy of Sciences, Brno

I Introduction

It has come to be widely recognized that the scientific and technological revolution in warfare, with its central product of nuclear weapons, and the current size of the nuclear arsenals of the world, combine to threaten both the destruction of human civilization and the functioning of the human environment. Other weapons of mass destruction and non-nuclear techniques of modifying the environment for hostile purposes are similarly seen as being perverse. However, a modern war could devastate the region in which it occurs even without resort to nuclear or other non-conventional weapons or methods.

Among the important concerns in a major modern war would be its secondary impact, one that derives from the anthropogenic component of the human environment: large human settlements, industrial complexes, chemical works, nuclear facilities, energy installations, fuel storage and supply systems, traffic networks, communication systems, intensive agricultural systems, and other elements typical of densely populated and highly industrialized societies. The effects of explosive, incendiary, and other conventional weapons could be highly amplified by: (a) chemical contamination, caused primarily by the destruction of storage tanks or chemical facilities or by the burning of various chemical products; and (b) by extensive and long-term radioactive contamination, caused by the destruction of nuclear-energy installations, reprocessing and nuclear-fuel plants, and nuclear-waste repositories (see Chapter 2). The combined effects could become comparable to those of chemical or nuclear weapons.

This chapter is devoted to an analysis of the dangerous forces that would be released into the environment (into the air, water,

---

[1] This chapter has been adapted by the editor from the author's more extensive symposium presentation.

and soil) following even conventional strikes on chemical facilities. Thus, examined here are the character and extent of effects on the environment by releases of harmful chemicals from: (a) destroyed or damaged production equipment; (b) destroyed or damaged storage and transport tanks; and (c) burning chemicals from exploded or ignited equipment and tanks. The present chapter builds upon prior work by the author (Matousek, 1980a; 1989).

II Peacetime Accidents in Chemical Facilities

The Chemical Industry of Today

The chemical industry of today is huge and scattered throughout many parts of the world (see Appendix 2). However, it does not under normal conditions contribute as much to environmental contamination as does agriculture, mining, or energy production. The production and handling of toxic or otherwise harmful chemicals – technologies that could be expected to be dangerous – have, in fact, contributed little to long-term environmental damage owing to the generally elaborate arrangements for work-place safety and environmental protection. However, the number of peacetime accidents is increasing and thus becomes a matter of increasing concern.

Throughout the world during the past three decades, direct property losses from accidents in the hydrocarbon chemical industry alone amounted to an estimated 3.5 thousand million dollars (US$ 1986) (Marshall, 1987). Four of the losses each exceeded 100 million dollars. Included were 99 accidents resulting from fire or explosion, 13 during the first decade, 28 during the second, and 58 during the third. These figures reflect only a part of the story. Some serious incidents may have escaped the public record entirely, since toxic incidents that produce little property damage are not likely to be listed even if fatalities are involved. Moreover, the figures include only direct losses.

Large-scale chemical disasters arise from two main factors, a high concentration of hazardous substances on a site or else the presence on a site of unusually hazardous substances – or from some combination of these two factors (Marshall, 1987).

The high concentration of hazardous substances on a single site has been increasing in prevalence because the increasing demand by society for petroleum and petrochemical products has been met far more by expansions in the production capacity of existing plants than by an increase in the numbers of small production units. For example, in the 1950s, sulfuric acid (H_2SO_4) was being produced largely by plants with a production capacity of ten tonnes per day, whereas today plants with a production capacity of 2000 tonnes per day are not uncommon. As an accompaniment to this trend, there has been a corresponding growth in the capacity of transport facilities, whether by road, rail, water, or pipeline.

The presence on a site of unusually hazardous substances has been increasing in prevalence because of a growing need for them in industry and also because the technology for handling them in relative safety has advanced (for example, dangerous gases are now being handled in safer liquid form).

The dangerous forces released in accidents at chemical facilities have predominantly acute or short-term effects, although delayed or long-term effects do occur in some instances. This is the case because the chemicals released become dispersed by air or water currents, and also because they usually decompose more or less rapidly through physical or microbiological action.

Accidents at Chemical Facilities

Peacetime accidents at chemical facilities can result from construction or material failures. They can be triggered by natural disasters (e.g., earthquakes, floods, lightning strikes) or human actions (e.g., faulty design, operating errors, sabotage).

Major accidents involving chemical facilities – including production, storage, and transport equipment – fall into a number of categories (Matousek, 1980a):

1 *Leakages* of hazardous chemicals – which lead to a release into the atmosphere of gases of toxic, inflammable, or explosive chemicals from a point source (either stationary or moving);

2 *Explosions* of hazardous chemicals – which lead both to a blast wave and to releases into the atmosphere of greater or lesser amounts of toxic, inflammable, or explosive chemicals;

3 *Fires* of hazardous or non-hazardous chemicals or materials – which lead both to fire damage and to releases into the atmosphere of clouds of toxic and non-toxic gases, particles, and other products of combustion; and

4 *Failures* of air-cleaning or water-cleaning systems – which lead to releases into the atmosphere or water of toxic chemicals.

Generally speaking, the potential for injury to humans and other biota is higher in connection with atmospheric releases than with releases into the water.

The accidental release of phosgene gas ($COCl_2$) into the atmosphere from the Müggenburg chemical plant in Hamburg on 20 May 1928 led to important early technical studies of the spread of such a contaminant in the atmosphere (Gillert, 1943; Matousek, 1980a). In that accident, a tank containing ten tonnes of phosgene ruptured, releasing a toxic plume that diffused in a southwesterly direction. There happened to be five people out in the open in the zone of the diffusion plume within 450 meters of the plant, all of whom were killed. Between 450 and 2000 meters there occurred a further six deaths as well as 20 serious and 50 light casualties. At a distance of 2000 to 7000 meters, approximately

130 persons were lightly wounded. Traces of the gas could be detected as far away as 14 kilometers.

Had the phosgene released in the Müggenburg accident diffused from its point source in the form of an ideal half-cone, toxic levels would not have reached the distance they did. In fact, a subsequent assessment and re-enactment of the Müggenburg accident established that the plume diffused in the form of a deformed half-cone having a horizontal (lateral) spread of 30° and vertical spread of 15°, with the angle of lateral spread remaining steady, but with the angle of vertical spread diminishing after reaching an altitude of about 50 meters (Gillert, 1943; Matousek, 1980a). However, experience from more recent chemical releases suggests that the lateral angle of diffusion of gases released into the atmosphere is more nearly 40° than 30°.

A disaster that occurred at the Hoffmann-La Roche chemical plant in Seveso, Italy on 10 July 1976 resulted in a major release of 2,4,5-trichlorophenol (contaminated with perhaps 2.5 kilograms of 2,3,7,8-tetrachlorodibenzo-*para*-dioxin) (Homberger *et al.*, 1979; Matousek, 1980a; Reggiani, 1978). Such dioxin, a super-toxic agent possessing mutagenic, teratogenic, and embryo-toxic properties, is usually formed upon the combustion of poly-halogenated aromatic compounds. It is thus a widespread potential danger at fires in chemical facilities.

The most disastrous recent chemical release occurred at the Union Carbide plant in Bhopal, India on 3 December 1984 (Bowonder *et al.*, 1985; Matousek, 1988; Nefedov & Yegorov, 1986). The plant was producing the insecticide 1-naphthyl-*N*-methylcarbamate ('Arylam', 'Sevin') from methyl isocyanate, a highly dangerous (toxic, inflammable, and reactive) chemical. A small volume of water was introduced into a storage tank containing about 45 cubic meters of the methyl isocyanate. The resulting exothermic reaction ruptured the tank, permitting the unreacted methyl isocyanate to escape under high pressure. This toxic cloud traversed a densely populated area and caused some 2300 early fatalities plus 30 000 to 40 000 serious injuries.

The Lessons Learned

The results of accidents, experiments, and modelling in recent years have provided a number of important lessons with regard to safety and warning systems, training of personnel, amounts of highly hazardous substances to store, and plant location (Ooms & Tennekes, 1984; Seinfeld, 1986). The great importance of meteorological conditions has been recognized. The toxicity of the released chemical has been shown to play a decisive role especially if the agent is a highly toxic, low-volatile one (e.g., a systemic pesticide). The Seveso accident was a case in point.

The most important properties of potentially dangerous industrial chemicals turn out to be their toxicity, their boiling point, and their

Table 3.1   *Common industrial chemicals with properties that indicate their potential danger*

Chemical compound	Toxicity of vapor in air	Boiling point (°C)	Potential for flashing
Ammonia (NH_3)	Low	−33	Moderate
Carbon disulfide (CS_2)	Very low	46	None
Chlorine (Cl_2)	High	−35	Moderate
Formaldehyde (HCHO)	Moderate	−21	Moderate
Hydrogen chloride (HCl)	Low	−85	High
Hydrogen cyanide (HCN)	High	26	Low
Hydrogen fluoride (HF)	High	20	Low
Hydrogen sulfide (H_2S)	High	−61	High
Nitrogen dioxide (NO_2)	High	21	None
Phosgene ($COCl_2$)	High	8	Low
Phosphorus trichloride (PCl_3)	Moderate	76	None
Sulfur dioxide (SO_2)	Moderate	−10	Moderate

Sources and notes: Boiling points are at normal atmospheric pressure (101 kilopascals) (Weast & Astle, 1979–1980, pp. B50–B144,C309), the lower the more potentially dangerous. The potential for flashing is the potential for the agent to vaporize with great rapidity if released rapidly from storage as a liquid under pressure. Table prepared by A.H. Westing.

ability to flash (see Table 3.1).[2] Liquified gases which can flash are very dangerous even if they are not highly toxic (Marshall, 1987). For example, thousands of tonnes of chlorine (Cl_2) or ammonia (NH_3) are often stored under pressure, constituting a potentially very serious problem.[3] Propane ($CH_3CH_2CH_3$) provides another example. At a storage temperature of 24°C, propane exerts a pressure of about 900 kilopascals. If the storage vessel is breached, the pressure will drop rapidly to atmospheric level, that is, to about 100 kilopascals, and the temperature will drop to about −42°C. The theoretical flashing fraction would be about 0.35, but in fact, much of the liquid would be expelled with explosive violence into the air as droplets. Chlorine and ammonia would behave in similar fashion.

After a chemical agent flashes, the resulting cloud of vapor (assuming that it is heavier than air, the usual situation) will at first be hemispherical in shape, but will soon form a plume moving downwind in the shape of a deformed half-cone. The shape, size, and direction

[2] When a vessel is breached that contains a volatile agent being stored under pressure (especially gases in liquid form), a portion of the agent will vaporize very rapidly, a phenomenon known as 'flashing'. Moreover, the temperature of the agent will at the same time decrease to its boiling point at atmospheric pressure.

[3] An often overlooked potential danger comes from the ammonia used in cooling systems associated with food-processing plants and ice-skating rinks that depend upon artificial ice. In Czechoslovakia alone there are more than 200 such ice-skating rinks that each store at least five tonnes of ammonia under pressure.

of plume depend not only upon the physical properties of the vapor, but also upon wind and other weather conditions and the nature of the terrain. However, as suggested earlier, for purposes of estimation the lateral angle of spread can be taken to be 40°, with the concentration diminishing symmetrically toward the edges of the plume (or, more precisely, with the lateral concentration profile taking the form of a Gaussian distribution). The effective length of the plume depends not only upon the toxicity, amount, and physical properties of the agent released, but also to a great extent upon wind velocity and other atmospheric conditions (vertical stability, presence of temperature inversions, etc.). The effective length of plume of chemicals that are dangerous owing primarily to their inflammability is usually shorter than that of toxic plumes because dilution often makes them more quickly innocuous. Obstructions such as trees and buildings might reduce the effective length of plume by two-thirds (Matousek, 1980a).

In the event that inflammable chemicals are released, the fires that are likely to result will release toxic fumes. The most severe of these chemical fires result from the ignition of clouds of inflammable vapors that give rise to fireballs. For example, if 20 tonnes of propane were to be rapidly released, ignition of the resulting cloud of vapor would produce a fireball with a diameter of about 125 meters that burns for about ten seconds. About one-third of the energy emitted during this brief time would be radiated at a level lethal to humans out to a distance of perhaps 50 meters from the fireball.

Explosions of solids or liquids are relatively rare in chemical plants outside the explosive industry. On the other hand, explosions of confined gases have long been relatively common occurrences. Explosions of vapor clouds are a more recent phenomenon, none having been known to occur prior to the 1940s. Such open-air vapor-cloud explosions proceed through an initial fireball that then explodes. Factors that favor such an escalation from fireball to explosion include greater lability and reactivity of the chemical, the presence of oxidative compounds, and partial confinement of the vapor cloud. One industrial explosion of this sort is reported to have destroyed all the buildings on an area of four hectares, at the same time killing more than 200 people (Marshall, 1987).

It is interesting to note that the ability for some chemical vapors to form fireballs that explode – for example, those of ethylene oxide (C_2H_4O) – has been exploited for weapon purposes, the so-called fuel/air explosive munitions (Matousek, 1980b).

III Wartime Releases of Dangerous Forces from Chemical Facilities

The potentially most dangerous triggering mechanism for the release of dangerous forces from chemical facilities is via military attack.

Whether a chemical plant is attacked intentionally or not, conventional weapons have become sufficiently destructive to be able to cause major leakages, explosions, and fires.

The extent of subsequent impact on humans in the area and on the surrounding environment would depend upon a number of factors, among them: (a) the type and quantity of weapons employed and their targeting success; (b) the type of chemical facility, the status of its chemical stocks, and the nature of its safety features; (c) the availability of damage-control personnel and equipment; (d) the local demographic and environmental characteristics; and (e) the meteorological conditions at the time of attack.

Modern conventional weapons are dangerous not only because of improvements in their destructiveness, but also because of improvements in their delivery systems. It is highly likely that chemical facilities would be attacked in any future war, whether or not this had been an intentional part of the strategy. This is so in part because there exist so many large and small chemical plants throughout the world (see Appendix 2). High concentrations of chemical facilities are often found in major river valleys and in major coal basins. Other concentrations of chemical plants are associated with oil or gas pipeline termini.

IV Conclusion

It appears certain the impact of even conventional weapons in an industrialized and densely populated region would be characterized by an amplification of injurious effects on humans and the environment owing to the release of dangerous chemicals, whether intentional or unintentional, from chemical facilities. Thus, the damage from a major conventional war could approach the damage that would result from a war in which chemical or nuclear weapons were employed.

The acute or short-term impact on humans and the environment in a major conventional war might well be dominated by chemicals released from the numerous chemical facilities likely to sustain damage. By contrast, the long-term and delayed impact would probably be dominated by radioactive contaminants released from the nuclear facilities that could also be expected to sustain damage.

It thus becomes clear that the prevention of nuclear or chemical war no longer suffices for the avoidance of human and environmental catastrophes. Such prevention must now be extended to include *all* war, in both industrialized and industrializing countries.

References

Bowonder, B., Kasperson, J.X., & Kasperson, R.E. 1985. Avoiding future Bhopals. *Environment*, Washington, 27(7):6–13,31–37.

Gillert, E. 1943. *Kampfstoffverletzungen [Chemical-warfare-agent injuries]* (in German). Berlin: Urban & Schwarzenberg, 120 pp.

Homberger, E., Reggiani, G., Sambeth, J., & Wipf, H.K. 1979. Seveso accident: its nature, extent and consequences. *Annals of Occupational Hygiene*, Oxford, 22:327–370.

Marshall, V. 1987. Major chemical hazards. *Scientific World*, London, 31(3):15–17.

Matousek, J. 1980a. [Accidents in chemical industry with release of harmful gases and vapors into the environment] (in Czech). *Obrana Vlasti*, Prague, 12(3):47–51.

Matousek, J. 1980b. [New munitions with an enhanced blast-wave effect] (in Czech). *Obrana Vlasti*, Prague, 12(1):33–39.

Matousek, J. 1988. [Bhopal: largest industrial disaster in recent years] (in Czech). *Obrana Vlasti*, Prague, 20(6):17–21.

Matousek, J. 1989. Impact on the social environment of a war with 'conventional' weapons. *Scientific World*, London, 33(1):14–18. [Summary in: *New Perspectives*, Helsinki, 19(4):6–7.]

Nefedov, O., & Yegorov, M. 1986. Multinationals in developing countries: lessons of the Bhopal tragedy. *Scientific World*, London, 30(3):19–22.

Ooms, G., & Tennekes, H. (eds). 1984. *Atmospheric dispersion of heavy gases and small particles*. West Berlin: Springer-Verlag, 440 pp.

Reggiani, G. 1978. Medical problems raised by the TCDD contamination in Seveso, Italy. *Archives of Toxicology*, West Berlin, 40:161–188.

Seinfeld, J.H. 1986. *Atmospheric chemistry and physics of air pollution*. New York: John Wiley, 738 pp.

Weast, R.C., & Astle, M.J. (eds). 1979–1980. *CRC handbook of chemistry and physics*. 60th ed. Boca Raton, Florida: CRC Press, [2447] pp.

4

The Release in War of Dangerous Forces from Hydrological Facilities

Margareta Bergström
Swedish Ministry of Defence

I Introduction

Catastrophic collapses of dams and dikes are able to occur in peacetime as well as in wartime. Although the causes of such events may differ in peace and in war, consequences and possible protective measures would be much the same. Therefore, peacetime experience with dam catastrophes – whether with preventive or damage-limitation measures – can provide important lessons for emergency planning in the event of war. The present chapter thus draws upon both peacetime and wartime experiences of dam catastrophes. It builds especially upon investigations in Sweden by the author and others (e.g., Bergström & Dreborg, 1984; Gustavsson *et al.*, 1984; Persson *et al.*, 1987; Svahn *et al.*, 1987).

II Background

Dams and dikes are built for various purposes. Drinking-water, irrigation, and flood-control dams have been constructed in many countries throughout history. More recently, dams have also been built for hydroelectric power and recreational purposes. The numbers of dams and their sizes have grown substantially during the present century, thereby increasing the potential for secondary destruction, should the dams collapse.

The importance of dams and dikes to society, as well as the enormous forces that could be released if they were to be destroyed, make them potential targets in wartime. In the event that both adversaries in a war were to possess potentially dangerous dams, a fear of retaliation in kind might introduce at least some element of restraint in targeting them. Another reason for restraint is that these objects are to some extent protected by international law (see Appendices 3.5 & 3.6). A reason for restraint with reference to hydroelectric dams is that if the purpose of the attack is to disrupt an enemy's electrical system, the latter could be more effectively disrupted by other means.

It is important to point out that the systems that regulate the flow of water are themselves vulnerable to disruption. If such systems were to malfunction during a period of high-water conditions – whether in time of peace or war, and whether by accident or intent – they could cause the destruction of a dam that leads in turn to catastrophic flooding.

Dam catastrophes can result from such events as: (a) a flood wave resulting from large masses falling into the water upstream from the dam; (b) unexpectedly heavy rainfall or snow melt; (c) an earthquake; (d) a breakdown of electrical or telecommunication systems involved in the operation of the dam; (e) a lack of monitoring or maintenance; (f) a lack of emergency planning or resources; and (g) sabotage or overt attack. In many cases, a combination of several of these factors constitutes the difference between a harmless incident and a large-scale accident.

III Peacetime Dam Accidents

Many countries regard information on large dams as sensitive. Published figures on dams, as on dam accidents, are therefore incomplete. Two important bodies exist that work towards the improvement of dam security, the International Commission on Large Dams (Paris) and the United Nations Disaster Relief Co-ordinator (Geneva).

There are more than 777 dams in the world that are at least 15 meters in height and impound at least 500 million cubic meters of water (see Appendix 2). Obviously, size of dam and impoundment are not the only factors that can contribute to a major accident. Very important additional factors are the regional topography and the demography below the dam. Flood-control dams are often relatively low structures situated in densely populated lowland areas. Hydroelectric dams are often relatively high structures in sparsely populated upland (mountainous) areas, although the collapse of such dams in some instances does threaten large cities.

Reports of dam accidents generally focus on such immediate effects as volume of water released, speed of the flood-wave, extent of area temporarily flooded, and number of casualties. However, of additional importance would be information on such factors as loss of topsoil (leading to reduction in agricultural potential), disruption of regional or even national supply of electricity, and regional non-habitability. In the case of war, dam and other reconstruction could be delayed for many years.

There have been well over 100 major dam failures during the past century, a considerable proportion of these having occurred at first filling (ICOLD, 1974). Outline descriptions of six accidents from among dams higher than 15 meters, instructive for one reason or another, follow (Svahn *et al.*, 1987, pp. 74–82):

1 *Vega de Tera, Spain, January 1959:* A 34 meter high concrete dam spanning the Tera River collapsed, resulting in the escape of 8 million cubic meters of water within 20 minutes (ICOLD, 1974, pp. 64–67,428–431). The mountain village of Rivaldelago, 5 kilometers downstream, was destroyed and 144 people killed. The break had begun in a joint between concrete and masonry at one of the edges of the dam, following unusually heavy rains.

2 *Malpasset dam, France, December 1959:* A 66 meter high concrete vault dam spanning the Revan River collapsed, releasing a significant fraction of the 22 million cubic meters of impounded water (ICOLD, 1974, pp. 33–40,393–396). Great damage was incurred over the 11 kilometers down to the Mediterranean Sea, destroying the town of Fréjus and killing 421 persons. Failure was attributed to weakness in the underlying bedrock.

3 *Vaiont (Vajont) dam, Italy, October 1963:* A great rock slide into the reservoir of a 266 meter high concrete arch dam spanning the Vaiont River resulted in huge waves, which – although they did not damage the integrity of the dam – swept 115 million cubic meters of water over the top (ICOLD, 1974, pp. 75–82,935–938). Five villages were destroyed and 2600 people killed. The accident occurred following unusually heavy rains.

4 *Frias, Argentina, January 1970:* A 15 meter high rock and concrete dam spanning the Mendoza River washed away owing to a fierce rain storm. A 2 meter high wave swept over a nearby city, destroying the homes of more than 500 people and killing 40.

5 *Teton, Idaho, USA, June 1976:* A 93 meter high earthen dam spanning the Snake River collapsed during the first filling, releasing 300 million cubic meters of water. The people living downstream (in Teton and Sugar City) were able to be warned, which substantially limited casualties, with only 11 people being killed. The failure was attributed to a deficiency in design.

6 *Noppikoski, Sweden, September 1985:* A 16 meter high earthen dam spanning the Ore River was partly washed away after a regulating door became stuck, emptying its 3 million cubic meter reservoir within 45 minutes. The malfunctioning was attributed to very heavy rains that caused the river to exceed substantially its estimated maximum flow. The river dug itself a new channel for 2 kilometers. Three bridges were damaged and woodlands were levelled, but no person was hurt.

IV Wartime Dam Destruction

A spectacular example of wartime dam attacks is provided by the Allied bombing of three major dams in the Ruhr valley of Germany in World War II, part of the Allied strategy of economic warfare, with special reference to the German arms industry. These were the

Möhne, Eder, and Sorpe – the last of which, however, was only lightly damaged.

The Möhne reservoir, with a capacity of 130 million cubic meters, had a decisive importance for electrical supply in the Ruhr valley and also for water regulation there. The Möhne and Sorpe dams together provided the industries in the Ruhr valley and the 4.5 million inhabitants there with water, flood protection, and electricity. The Eder dam regulated water flow in the Mittelland Canal, at the same time providing electricity and flood protection to its valley. The Allied (British) plan had been to empty the three dams simultaneously in order to bring to a standstill all of the Ruhr industries.

Upon being breached in May 1943, the Möhne and Eder dams (each stone-filled concrete structures about 40 meters high) released perhaps 120 million and 150 million cubic meters of water, respectively, the one in 12 hours and the other in 36 (Brickhill, 1951; Kirschmer, 1949; Meyer, 1948; Quast, 1949; see also Chapter 1). During the first hour, the breach in the Möhne dam released 9000 cubic meters of water. The flood wave was ten meters high and moved at a speed of seven meters per second. The flood waters adversely affected the entire Ruhr valley, including such important cities as Dortmund, Düsseldorf, and Essen. Had the Sorpe dam (a 69 meter high, earthen dam with concrete membrane) been destroyed as well, the consequences for the Ruhr valley might well have been immeasurable (ICOLD, 1974, p. 520).

The attacks were considered a great success by the Allies. The immediate effects were enormous, severely reducing the working capacity in the Ruhr valley, and bringing about a major human tragedy. There were more than 1300 dead, and 120 000 were made homeless. Some 3000 hectares of arable land were ruined and 25 water treatment plants destroyed. Many coal mines were flooded and 125 factories and 12 power stations destroyed or badly damaged. Destroyed as well were seven dams, 11 highway bridges, four railroad bridges, and 30 kilometers of railroad track. Long after the dams were repaired, the valley below remained littered with twisted, rusting girders and huge lumps of concrete, and the earth continued to look as though a giant rake had scoured it.

It could be argued that huge reservoirs built for the production of electricity should be emptied during wartime if there were a risk of bombing. This might be especially attractive in the case of large concrete arch dams, which are more vulnerable to destruction than earthen dams (the Sorpe dam being a case in point). However, it does not seem generally feasible to do so in advance because the electricity being produced will be needed; nor is it feasible at the time when an attack seems imminent because it would generally take several days to do so.

V Disruption of the Supply of Electricity

The supply of electricity is vulnerable to disruption in a modern society; and, in turn, such vulnerability accounts in part for the vulnerability of other societal systems – especially so under wartime conditions. Thus, in a modern society, disruption of the supply of electricity can be regarded a major aim for an attacker, especially in the vulnerable mobilization phase of the attacked nation, a period during which dependency of military forces on the regular electrical network would be high. Such disruption could also be decisive in disrupting industrial capacity during the latter phases of a war of attrition. Still, it would seem to be generally more cost-effective for the attacker to target other parts of the system than dams or power stations (whether by air or by sabotage), for instance, transforming plants or other key nodes.

In the case of a surprise attack, a rather limited amount of sabotage could disrupt the interconnected electrical system of a highly industrialized nation on a regional to national scale. This would not only slow down mobilization, but would also disrupt societal life in general. The destruction of well-chosen transforming plants could keep the system non-functional for several months or longer (Bergström & Dreborg, 1984, pp. 25–51). National vulnerability of this sort has increased enormously since World War II, making the experience of that war in part outdated.

The case of Sweden is illustrative. The Swedish national electrical network is designed for high reliability. In fact, reliability is generally considered to be so high that even critically dependent users often lack an alternative source of energy. One of its special features is the combination of hydroelectric power (produced mostly in the north) and nuclear power (produced mostly in the south), each accounting for about half of the national total. Most people live in the southern portion of the country, so that much electricity is moved from north to south. The system is meshed so that several routings are possible.

However, even small-scale sabotage on a key node could cause severe disruption on a nationwide scale that lasts for hours or days. This was well demonstrated by a recent accident.

On 27 December 1983, a switching device in the switch-yard at Hamra became overheated (Persson et al., 1987). As a consequence, a temporary connection was established between the two normally separated halves of the switch-yard. The transmission load was already extremely high at the time, owing to a shutdown in a nuclear power plant half an hour earlier. The overheated switching device collapsed, causing a power failure. The temporary connection between the two halves of the Hamra switch-yard led to the simultaneous tripping of two 400 kilovolt lines from the north. The loss of Hamra led in turn to the overloading of another line, followed by a voltage collapse after about one minute, which resulted in the tripping of all transmission lines between northern and central Sweden. The rapid changes in frequency and voltage made it impossible for the nuclear plants to continue their production of electricity.

Power was out for most users throughout Sweden for one to seven hours. Restoration work was delayed by incidents such as the blocking of telephone lines. Another problem was that the power and transmission plants that had shut down depended for their start-up on systems that required the very electricity that had become unavailable. In wartime, such an accident would probably leave the entire country dark for a much longer period than in peacetime, and thus could severely disturb the war effort.

The Hamra blackout led to an investigation into the vulnerability of the electrical supply system in Sweden (Gustavsson et al., 1984). One part of the investigation was a review of the consequences of a shortfall of electricity in different sectors of society, among them, hospitals, public transportation, gasoline stations, water supplies, sewage systems, heating, milk production, food storage and preparation, electronic systems (computers, radios, telecommunications), and industrial production (Gustavsson et al., 1984, pp. 112–141). Serious vulnerabilities were found in several instances, some of which had been unexpected. For example, the vulnerability of electrical heating to a loss of electricity is obvious. Less well known was that almost all modern heating systems rely on electricity for some essential function, for example, the operation of circulation pumps. In fact, for a highly urbanized country like Sweden, the situation for the civilian population would become very difficult if the supply of electricity should be broken off for more than 24 hours. Although hardship must be accepted in wartime, there would be few alternatives to electric power distributed through a national network to keep in operation activities essential to the war effort.

One of the most important lessons from the Hamra accident was the extent to which unforeseen coincidences affected the outcome of the event.

VI Dam Security: The Example of Sweden

Given the great importance of hydroelectric power in the energy system of Sweden, given the great number of its dams (thousands, large and small), and given the great weight Sweden has traditionally placed on all aspects of security, Swedish dam security is a good starting point for an analysis of the hazards connected with dams, whether in reference to peace or war. Indeed, a series of incidents during the 1980s initiated substantial security work in Sweden.

The Swedish rivers used for power production have a rather limited falling height over most of their extent. To make possible the sustained production of electricity, a complex system of large reservoirs has had to be built, by means of which the water flow of the whole river – through plants and regulated by dams – must be carefully managed.

Several great rivers flow from the mountains in the border region between Sweden and Norway to the northern Baltic Sea. A series of dams and power plants has been built there. The most important river system in this respect is the Lule, which accounts for nearly 25% of all the hydroelectric power generated in Sweden. The Lule River system (the Great Lule and the Little Lule, joining to form the Lule) supports several reservoirs and 15 power plants.

A dam must contain openings that can be varied in size for the purpose of regulating water flow and level. In Sweden, most dams operate automatically. Such automatic regulation must be highly reliable to minimize the risk of flooding. In the ever more complex power systems along major rivers, where reservoir volumes are small compared with the flow of water, the automatic regulating systems must be highly sophisticated. It is essential that a back-up power supply is provided for, should the network fail.

Swedish Dam Accidents

The largest impoundment on the Great Lule River is the Suorva reservoir, created by three separate earthen dams (Persson *et al.*, 1987). It consists of a lake system having a surface area of 26 000 hectares and a capacity of 6×10^9 cubic meters (30 to 60 times more than the above-described Möhne and Eder impoundments destroyed during World War II). From the Suorva reservoir, water is directed down through nine major power plants along the Lule River, together accounting for 10% of the electrical production of Sweden.

In October 1983, a leak was discovered in the eastern dam (Persson *et al.*, 1987). This dam, which had been constructed during 1968 to 1972, was regarded as unbreakable. It is about 720 meters long, 50 meters high, and 1.3 million cubic meters in volume (filled with earth and rock). When the leak was discovered, the flow through it was 8 cubic meters per minute. The following day, a cavity of 30 cubic meters was discovered near the crest of the dam, the result of subsequently discovered undermining.

The breached dam had not been built to allow for over-flooding. Therefore, when the leak was discovered, the level of the water had to be lowered. The Lule River valley is 320 kilometers long and supports four communities having a total population of 130 000 people, a majority of whom live or work close to the river. In the worst case, the waters could flush down the valley at 15 kilometers per hour. It was primarily as a consequence of the Suorva leak (but also of the later Noppikoski accident) that extensive contingency studies were initiated by the Swedish government (Svahn *et al.*, 1987).

A probable consequence of the total destruction of a Suorva dam would be the washing out of all of the downstream dams and the destruction of many downstream bridges. The flooding would disrupt road and train traffic downstream. The telecommunication network might break down, and energy supply would be seriously interrupted. The regional municipal water systems, all of which are dependent upon the river, would remain unusable for a long time.

Many societal functions would break down as a direct or indirect result of the flood wave and remain disrupted for a lengthy period of time. The flood waters themselves can be expected to persist for about two weeks, and subsequent restoration efforts would be a slow process.

Swedish Emergency Planning
Several river valleys in Sweden are very sensitive to floods, whether owing to excessive rain or to dam breakage (Persson *et al.*, 1987). A system for water-flow forecasts (assisted by a network of metering points, automatically reported to a computer) has been created by the Swedish National Institute for Meteorology and Hydrology, and a rescue service is to be alerted when there is risk of high water.

Swedish dams were examined extensively for possible weaknesses following the Suorva leak. A computerized dam register, covering about 1000 dams, is being set up that contains relevant information, including estimates of maximum water volume that might be released in the event of breaching. New construction norms are in preparation that provide for larger gates for the emergency release of water. Some additional dikes have been built.

The recent dam and flooding accidents have demonstrated that the unthinkable is possible even in this area, and thus have accentuated the need for estimating the consequences of a major accident and for the preparation of emergency plans. Such plans must provide for: (a) technical measures, for example, automatic water-level monitoring; (b) an organizational structure; (c) evacuation of threatened inhabitants; (d) sheltering; and (e) rescue equipment.

Sweden has specific laws that regulate construction, use, and maintenance of dams, placing it among the very few countries with such legislation. Sweden also has rather advanced emergency plans, which could serve as a model to other countries. Potential dam accidents should be studied, emergency plans developed, and responses rehearsed. Plans that deal with accidents that cover several communities are to be worked out by the appropriate county government. Moreover, all of the plans are worked out in conjunction with military authorities, to be equally useful in times of peace and war. Most Swedish dams function automatically, but in time of war present plans call for technicians to be assigned, as necessary, to such installations.

It is important that the established rescue service gets adequate information as soon as an accident happens, and that it can quickly summon relevant personnel and alert the population. The result of all this preparation has been that plans should now exist in Sweden for all communities where these risks prevail. The most extensive emergency plans have been prepared by the communities along the Lule River (Persson *et al.*, 1987, pp. 15–17). For example, in Boden, up to 15 000 persons would have to be evacuated in the event of a dam failure since the main part of the community would become inundated. The emergency planning allows for evacuation within 20 hours. In Luleå, a plan has been developed in conjunction with the military authorities for the evacuation of 60 000 people.

It is clear that targeting of the dams themselves is not necessary to cause dams to collapse in time of war. They could be made to collapse, whether intentionally or inadvertently: (a) if the flow of water upstream from the dam were substantially increased; (b) if weaknesses in the construction of the dam became indirectly aggravated; or (c) if the flow-regulating system were caused to malfunction. The last possibility seems especially likely.

Wartime accidents will not necessarily be more drastic than peace-time ones. On the contrary, in wartime certain routine precautions are often taken to lessen the potential impact of a disaster – at least in the Swedish plans – such as lowering the water level of reservoirs. Moreover, Swedish safety norms for dams take into account the risk of war. For example, dam size is intentionally made more massive to allow for conventional bombing to a certain extent.

Past experience with dam failures, present monitoring systems, flood-simulation computer programs, and existing contingency plans together now appear adequate to prevent a catastrophe in Sweden in the event of a dam accident in peacetime. However, the chaos that may characterize a wartime situation emphasizes the importance that firm provisions be made not only for detailed emergency plans, but also for reliable monitoring systems, back-up power supplies, and dependable telecommunication networks.

VII Conclusion

It is clear that dam catastrophes, with their enormous potential for destroying both humans and their supporting environment, are possible both in times of war and peace. It must also be stressed again that dam catastrophes can occur even if the dam itself is not attacked or otherwise damaged. A number of recommendations are thus in order:

1 The attacking of dams is restricted by international law (see Appendices 3.5 & 3.6; see also Chapters 5 & 6). Dams could be attacked nevertheless or else destroyed indirectly. International law should be strengthened in this regard, and more nations should be urged to become party to the relevant treaties. The international community should react strongly to any violations. Moreover, electricity is so extremely important to the well-being of the civilian population of

modern societies, that even attacks on the national electrical supply system as such could cause such severe effects on the population that there should be restrictions on attacking these as well.

2 Although dams have been built for many years, recent experience in Sweden shows that better design and construction methods are needed. It is important that these new methods be applied not only to the construction of new dams, but also to the improvement of existing dams.

3 Each country should establish an independent surveillance authority for dam security. Operating and monitoring systems should be designed to take into account the possibility of wartime conditions, especially with respect to electrical supply, communication systems, and transportation. Wartime plans must include provisions for the lowering of reservoir water levels and for the shutting down of nuclear power plants. Finally, a contingency plan is needed for the rationing of electricity.

The supply of electricity was disrupted during World War II largely as a side effect of bombing nearby industries. However, postwar evaluations have made it clear that neither the importance nor the vulnerability of power production and distribution systems (especially of transforming stations) had been sufficiently appreciated by either side. Such an oversight is not likely to be repeated in a future war.

References

Bergström, M., & Dreborg, K.-H. 1984. *Säkerhetspolitiska hot mot fredssamhället [sic: Security politics threat against the peaceful society]* (in Swedish). Stockholm: Swedish Ministry of Defence, 91 pp.

Brickhill, P. 1951. *Dam busters.* London: Evans Brothers, 269 pp. + 13 plates.

Gustavsson, B., *et al.* 1984. *Säker elförsörjning [Secure electrical supply]* (in Swedish). Stockholm: Statens Offentliga Utredningar No. SOU 1984:69, 283 pp.

ICOLD. 1974. *Lessons from dam incidents.* Paris: International Commission on Large Dams, 1069 pp.

Kirschmer, O. 1949. [Destruction and protection of dams and dikes] (in German). *Schweizerische Bauzeitung* (now *Schweizer Ingenieur & Architekt*), Zürich, 67:277–281,300–303.

Meyer, E. 1948. [Fundamentals regarding the choice of type of dam wall for large reservoirs] (in German). *Schweizerische Bauzeitung* (now *Schweizer Ingenieur & Architekt*), Zürich, 66:150–152.

Persson, C.G., *et al.* 1987. *Läckaget i suorvadammen i Oktober 1983 [The leak in the Suorva dam in October 1983]* (in Swedish). Stockholm: Ministry of Defence, Utredningsrapport No. 1:1987, 27 pp. + 7 appendices.

Quast, H. 1949. [Destruction and reconstruction of the Möhne and Eder dams] (in German). *Wasser- & Energiewirtschaft* (now *Wasser, Energie, Luft*), Baden, Switz., 41:135–139,149–154.

Svahn, H., *et al.* 1987. *Dammsäkerhet och skydd mot översvämningar [Dam safety and protection against flooding]* (in Swedish). Stockholm: Statens Offentliga Utredningar No. SOU 1987:64, 251 pp.

5

The Mitigation of Environmental Disruption by War: Legal Approaches

Jozef Goldblat

Geneva International Peace Research Institute

I Introduction

The humanitarian law of armed conflict contributes to the protection of the human environment, both directly and indirectly. Several international legal norms are specifically oriented towards the environment, and thus to a greater or lesser extent encompass the release of dangerous forces from such sources as nuclear, chemical, and hydrological facilities. Those instruments which have imposed constraints directly related to the conduct of war are described here. Proposals are also made for strengthening and developing them.

This chapter builds upon previous work by the author and others (Bothe *et al.*, 1982; Bring, 1987; Goldblat, 1982b; 1983; 1985; Sandoz *et al.*, 1987; Sims, 1981).

II Background

Efforts to reduce brutality in war, motivated by humanitarian, religious, and – above all – practical considerations, have a long history. A body of restrictions and limitations upon what states might do when at war has developed as customary law. During the second half of the 19th century, this customary law began to be supplemented by conventional law in the form of international multilateral agreements. Among these, the Declaration of St Petersburg of 1868 was of special significance: it proclaimed that the only legitimate objective of states during war is to weaken the military forces of the enemy (Goldblat, 1982a, pp. 120–121). Since then, the international humanitarian law of armed conflicts has developed in two broad streams: (a) rules relating to targets – those according protection to certain persons, places, objects, or the human environment in general – and (b) rules relating to specific weapons.

A major attempt to bring the two streams of law together into a mutually reinforcing relationship was made during the Diplomatic Conference on the Reaffirmation and Development of International

Humanitarian Law Applicable in Armed Conflicts, which was held in Geneva from 1974 to 1977. However, the agreements reached there and contained in Protocol I of 1977 on the Protection of Victims of International Armed Conflicts (see Appendix 3.5) deal exclusively with the 'target' stream of restrictions. As regards the 'weapon' stream, Protocol I has merely reaffirmed the general principles of international law already embodied in the regulations annexed to Hague Convention II of 1899 with Respect to the Laws and Customs of War on Land (see Appendix 3.1) or to Hague Convention IV of 1907 Respecting the Laws and Customs of War on Land (see Appendix 3.2). Protocol I has thus proclaimed that the right of the parties to an armed conflict to choose methods or means of warfare is not unlimited, and that it is prohibited to use weapons and methods of warfare that might cause superfluous injury or unnecessary suffering. The term 'methods and means of warfare' covers weapons in the broadest sense; no specific weapon has been expressly banned by Protocol I. Equally vague are the 'superfluous' and 'unnecessary' qualifications.

The 'weapon' stream – the centerpiece of which continues to be the ban on the use in war of chemical and biological weapons through the Geneva Protocol of 1925 on Chemical and Bacteriological Warfare (Goldblat, 1982a, pp. 135–136) – was complemented in 1977 by a prohibition on the hostile use of environmental modification techniques (see Appendix 3.4). In 1980, a convention prohibiting or restricting the use of certain 'inhumane' conventional weapons was added to this body of law (see Appendix 3.7; see also Goldblat, 1982a, pp. 296–302).

Various of the major multilateral agreements that serve in some fashion to protect the human environment in time of war are analyzed below in chronological order. These agreements are not only complex, but are limited by imprecisions of definition, formal and informal reservations, and varying levels of national commitment to adherence. The applicability of these agreements to disruption of the environment by dangerous forces released as a result of hostile actions is by no means straightforward.

III Relevant Multilateral Agreements

Geneva Protocol of 1925
The Geneva Protocol of 1925 on Chemical and Bacteriological Warfare (Goldblat, 1982a, pp. 135–136) was a protocol to the Geneva Convention of 1925 for the Supervision of the International Trade in Arms and Ammunition and in Implements of War, which did not itself enter into force. The Protocol prohibited the use in war of asphyxiating, poisonous, or other gases, and of all analogous liquids, materials, or devices, as well as the use of bacteriological methods of warfare. The Protocol, in force since 1928, actually restated – at least in the part dealing with gases – a prohibition previously declared in

various international documents, in particular, Hague Declaration 2 of 1899 banning the use of projectiles for the diffusion of asphyxiating or deleterious gases (Goldblat, 1982a, p. 121) and Hague Convention IV of 1907 banning the use of poison or poisoned weapons (Goldblat, 1982a, pp. 122–124, Annex Article XXIII.a). The need to reaffirm these bans was prompted by the experience of World War I, during which at least 125 000 tonnes of toxic chemicals were used and the toxic gas casualties exceeded by far one million.

The Geneva Protocol of 1925 is adhered to by over 100 nations, including all five permanent members of the United Nations Security Council. It can be considered deficient in that it restricts its non-use obligation: (a) to the conditions of 'war', instead of making it applicable to armed conflict in general; and (b) to relations 'as between' the parties, instead of being valid *vis-à-vis* all states. The Protocol has also been debilitated by reservations made by a number of states – among them, the five great powers – which limit its applicability to first use only, thereby preserving the option to retaliate with the weapons in question. However, the sharpest controversy has arisen over the scope of the prohibitions imposed by the Protocol.

Thus, there is the problem of irritants (such harassing agents as tear gas) that may be used in warfare, but which are also often employed for domestic law enforcement and riot control. An even greater dilemma, especially from the environmental point of view, is posed by the dual-purpose status of herbicides. For – apart from their peaceful applications in forestry, agriculture, and so forth – herbicides were extensively used during the Second Indochina War of 1961–1975, after having been first employed in Malaya during the 1950s (Westing, 1976; 1989). In 1969, the United Nations General Assembly declared as contrary to the generally recognized rules of international law the use in international armed conflicts of chemical agents of warfare, having a direct toxic effect not only on humans and animals, but also on plants (UNGA, 1969). However, the United Nations resolution did not receive unanimous support, and the controversy has remained unresolved.

In spite of its weaknesses, the Geneva Protocol of 1925 is a historic document. Its significance lies chiefly in the fact that an international legal constraint, 'binding alike the conscience and the practice of nations', was imposed on acts which were generally held in abhorrence and had been justly condemned by the general opinion of the civilized world. As regards biological and toxin weapons, the ban on their use has been reinforced by the Bacteriological and Toxin Weapon Convention of 1972, which prohibits the very possession of such weapons (Goldblat, 1982a, pp. 193–195).

Protocol I of 1977
Protocol I of 1977 on the Protection of Victims of International Armed Conflicts, additional to the Geneva Conventions of 1949 Relating to

Protection of Victims of Armed Conflicts, entered into force in 1978 (see Appendix 3.5). Protocol I has expanded the traditional rules regarding the protection of the civilian population and civilian objects in the conduct of military operations. In particular, there is a prohibition to carry out area bombing, to attack, by any means, undefended localities, or to extend military operations to zones on which the parties have conferred by agreement the status of demilitarized zone. Starvation has been banned as a method of warfare: it is prohibited to attack, destroy, remove, or render useless foodstuffs, agricultural areas for the production of foodstuffs, crops, livestock, drinking water installations and supplies, as well as irrigation works, for the specific purpose of denying them to the civilian population, whatever the motive of the attacker.

Protocol I of 1977 is meant to protect not only the population of the countries at war, but also the environment as such. A special article prohibits the use of methods and means of warfare that are intended or 'may be expected' to cause widespread, long-term, and severe damage to the natural environment. Battlefield damage incidental to warfare is not proscribed by this provision, but dams, dikes, and nuclear electric power-generating stations have been placed under special protection and must not be attacked if the result could be the release of dangerous forces causing severe losses among the civilian population. Even military objectives located in the vicinity of these installations must not be attacked if the same effects could result. To facilitate the identification of the relevant installations, the parties may use a special international sign.

Launching an attack against works and installations containing dangerous forces in the knowledge that such attack would cause excessive loss of life, injury to civilians, or damage to civilian objects, is to be regarded as a grave breach and, consequently, as a war crime, according to Protocol I of 1977. However, in an effort to halt or impede an advancing army, a party may destroy on its national territory the works and installations covered by the Protocol, and thereby release the dangerous forces contained therein, if the facilities in question are under its control at the time when the destruction is carried out. Similarly, an occupying power which has control of a given area, may carry out such destruction, if the act is rendered absolutely necessary by military operations. It is understood that in either case measures must be taken to ensure that the civilian population not be affected.

According to Protocol I of 1977, attacks against the natural environment by way of reprisal are prohibited. This prohibition is not subject to any condition and has a peremptory character.

Unfortunately, the reservations incorporated in the text of Protocol I of 1977 have reduced the practical value of many of its provisions. In several important instances, such as in the case of works and installations containing dangerous forces, derogation from the prohibitions may be made whenever it can be justified by 'military necessity'. However, the required justification is bound to be subjective, because there is no way of balancing such unquantifiable notions as human suffering and the demands of war. In practice, this proviso could amount to passing to commanders in the field the responsibility for deciding in the heat of battle what is lawful and what is not. Protocol I of 1977 has limited the introduction of new weapons by an article obliging the parties to determine – in the development and acquisition of such weapons – whether their employment would be prohibited by that Protocol or, indeed, by any other applicable rule of international law. However, such a determination of legality is not internationally binding.

It should be noted that, in addition to Protocol I of 1977, there exists a Protocol II of 1977 on the Protection of Victims of Non-International Armed Conflicts, which also entered into force in 1978 (see Appendix 3.6). Protocol II prescribes protection of civilians against the dangers arising from such conflicts and sets out minimum standards of humane treatment. It may thus help limit the means which could be used in internal wars, but situations of internal disturbances, such as riots and sporadic acts of violence, are not covered. Certain provisions of Protocol II coincide with those of Protocol I, but are more succinct. Installations containing dangerous forces are protected, without the exceptions specified in Protocol I, but the protection does not cover military objectives located at or near such installations.

Environmental Modification Convention of 1977
As distinct from the prohibitions of Protocol I of 1977, aimed at protecting the natural environment against damage that could be inflicted upon it by any weapon, the Environmental Modification Convention of 1977, in force since 1978, bans military or any other hostile use of environmental modification techniques as the means of destruction, damage, or injury (see Appendix 3.4). The techniques in question are those devised to change – through the deliberate manipulation of natural processes – the dynamics, composition, or structure of the earth, including its biota, lithosphere, hydrosphere, and atmosphere, or of outer space.

Whereas the relevant provisions of Protocol I of 1977 are applicable only when all three of the criteria – widespread, long-term, *and* severe – are met and the effects are cumulative, the Environmental Modification Convention of 1977 requires the presence of only one of the three criteria – widespread, long-lasting, *or* severe – for the environmental technique to be deemed outlawed. In addition, different meanings are suggested for the terms 'long-lasting' and 'long-term'. The first was defined – in an understanding worked out by the negotiators, although not written into the Environmental Modification Convention – as lasting for a period of months, or approximately a season (Goldblat,

1982a, pp. 230–231), whereas the latter was interpreted – during the Diplomatic Conference which drafted Protocol I of 1977 – as a matter of decades (Sandoz *et al.*, 1987, p. 446). However, the Convention does tolerate hostile uses of environmental modification techniques which produce destructive effects below the 'widespread, long-lasting or severe' threshold. Non-hostile uses are completely exempted from the prohibition, even if they produce destructive effects above the threshold. The described deficiencies may explain the low number of parties to the Convention, so far less than 60.

Inhumane Weapon Convention of 1980

In the context of humanitarian law, the term 'inhumane' sounds like a misnomer, because no weapon of war can be considered humane. There are, nevertheless, substantial differences in the effects that weapons produce. The differences regard, in particular, the magnitude, painfulness, and severity of the wounds, and the duration of the injury caused, as well as the extent of the geographical area covered and thereby the degree of the inflicted environmental damage.

The Inhumane Weapon Convention of 1980,[1] in force since 1983, prohibits or restricts the use of certain conventional weapons which may be deemed to be excessively injurious or have indiscriminate effects (see Appendix 3.7; see also Goldblat, 1982a, pp. 296–302; Westing, 1985, pp. 90–100). It has the format of an 'umbrella' treaty, under which specific agreements can be subsumed in the form of protocols. Three such protocols were agreed upon in the first instance, the latter two of which have environmental significance.

Protocol II of the Inhumane Weapon Convention of 1980 prohibits or restricts the use of mines, booby traps, and 'other devices' which are defined as manually emplaced munitions and devices designed to kill, injure, or damage, and which are actuated by remote control or automatically after a lapse of time. The use of all these weapons against the civilian population as such, or against individual civilians, is prohibited in all circumstances, whether in offense or defense or by way of reprisal. Also prohibited is their indiscriminate use against military objectives in conditions which may be expected to cause incidental loss of civilian life, injury to civilians, or damage to civilian objects – including, *inter alia*, croplands – excessive in relation to the concrete and direct military advantage anticipated. Booby traps designed to cause superfluous injury or unnecessary suffering are prohibited in all circumstances.

As regards the protection of the environment, Protocol II of the Inhumane Weapon Convention of 1980 is of special importance

---

[1] The Inhumane Weapon Convention was concluded in Geneva on 10 October 1980 and opened for signature in New York on 10 April 1981.

because it bans the use of remotely delivered mines – those delivered by artillery, rocket, mortar, or similar means, or dropped from an aircraft – unless such mines are only used within an area which is itself a military objective or which contains military objectives. Even then, the location of mines must be accurately recorded, or an effective neutralizing mechanism used to render the mines harmless or cause them to destroy themselves when they no longer serve the military purpose for which they were emplaced. Guidelines on recording the location of mine fields, mines, and booby traps are contained in an annex to Protocol II.

International cooperation in the removal of the devices in question after the cessation of hostilities is provided for in a separate article of Protocol II of the Inhumane Weapon Convention of 1980. A first major test of the working of this provision will be the expected removal of the mines laid down during the Afghan War of 1978–1988. Afghanistan has only signed the Inhumane Weapon Convention, whereas the USSR has been a party to it, including Protocol II, since 1982. In the case of the Gulf (Iran–Iraq) War of 1980–1988, the postwar handling of planted mines may present additional problems, because neither Iran nor Iraq was a party to the Convention.

As a matter of fact, not only mines but all explosive remnants of war scattered on land or at sea present a threat to the environment. Chemical components of certain unexploded munitions may have harmful effects on humans and animals, and even on the ecosystem as a whole.

Protocol III of the Inhumane Weapon Convention of 1980 restricts the use of incendiary weapons. Munitions that may have only an incidental incendiary effect, such as illuminants, tracers, smoke, or signalling systems, are excluded from the scope of Protocol III. The same exclusion applies to armor-piercing projectiles, fragmentation shells, explosive bombs, and similar combined-effect munitions in which the incendiary effect is not specifically intended to cause burn injury to persons, but is designed to set fire to such objects as armored vehicles, aircraft, and military installations or facilities.

The prohibitions and restrictions introduced by Protocol III of the Inhumane Weapon Convention of 1980 aim only at the protection of civilians. Thus, it is prohibited in all circumstances to make the civilian population as such, individual civilians or civilian objects, the object of attack by incendiary weapons. It is also prohibited to make a military objective situated within a concentration of civilians the object of attack by air-delivered incendiary weapons. None of the rules explicitly protects combatants. But even the protection of civilians is qualified in Protocol III: military objectives which are located within populated areas, but which are clearly separated from a concentration of civilians, are excluded from the restriction with respect to ground-delivered incendiary weapons. However, this Protocol does stipulate that all feasible precautions be taken in order to limit the incendiary effects to the military objective and to avoid or minimize incidental loss of civilian life, injury to civilians, and damage to civilian objects. 'Feasible precautions' are explained to mean precautions which are practicable or practically possible, taking into account all circumstances, 'including humanitarian and military considerations'.

It is important to note that observance of Protocol III of the Inhumane Weapon Convention of 1980 would mitigate the adverse impact of military activities on the natural environment (see Appendix 3.7). Attacks with incendiary weapons on forests or other kinds of plant cover are prohibited, except when such vegetation is used to cover, conceal, or camouflage combatants or other military objectives, or are themselves military objectives. Almost a decade after the conclusion of the Inhumane Weapon Convention, only about 30 countries have joined it. Most of the adherents have agreed to be bound by all three of its protocols (although acceptance of any two suffices for adherence).

IV Strengthening and Developing Humanitarian Law

Geneva Protocol of 1925

The Geneva Protocol of 1925 would be considerably reinforced by formal acceptance by all the parties of the comprehensive nature of the ban, in order to cover all chemical and biological methods of warfare without exception, and in all conflicts. However, the most important move would be the withdrawal of reservations limiting the applicability of the Protocol to nations party to it, and to first use only. This would amount to giving up the proclaimed right of second use; the prohibition would then become absolute and unconditional.

The suggested reinforcements of the Geneva Protocol of 1925 could be taken by way of unilateral statements or common understandings of the parties, without amending the text itself. In any event, it can be expected that they would be only transitional – until a convention prohibiting the possession of chemical weapons (complementing the Bacteriological and Toxin Weapon Convention of 1972 [Goldblat, 1982a, pp. 193–195]) would exclude their use under any circumstance.

Protocol I of 1977

The qualifications attached to the provisions of Protocol I of 1977 are imprecise enough to weaken the bans to which they are attached. This is particularly true regarding the prohibition on attacks against works and installations that are capable of releasing dangerous forces into the human environment, and which are likely to be primary targets in war. Indeed, the protection of such facilities may cease if they are used in 'significant and direct support' of military operations and if an attack on them is the only feasible way to terminate such support. However, the removal of these qualifications by amending Protocol I does not seem to be politically feasible. New international norms of behavior would be needed to impose a legal norm that unconditionally bans the use of force against these sensitive targets (see Chapter 6). In fact, the Protocol itself urges the contracting parties to conclude agreements ensuring additional protection of objects containing dangerous forces. To be more effective in reducing the danger of mass destruction, further prohibitions would have to be made unreservedly binding both on the attacker and on the defender.

The scope of a strengthened agreement would have to be broad enough to provide immunity to nuclear installations, especially reactors and plutonium separation plants, as well as to radioactive materials in transport or in storage, especially spent nuclear fuel and nuclear waste (see Chapter 2). Chemical factories, as well as toxic or otherwise dangerous substances in transport or in storage, would require comparable protection (see Chapter 3). Dams should be similarly provided with immunity (see Chapter 4). Moreover, 'scorched earth' actions, resulting in significant long-term damage for the country and its population, should not be allowed, even in defense against an invader.

Appropriate forums for these improvements include: (a) the Conference on Disarmament (Geneva), which is in the process of negotiating a chemical weapon convention and is considering the possibility of banning radiological warfare; and (b) the International Atomic Energy Agency (Vienna), under the auspices of which the 1980 Convention on the Physical Protection of Nuclear Material (Goldblat, 1982a, pp. 291–296) was concluded.

Environmental Modification Convention of 1977

The Environmental Modification Convention of 1977 is only a half-measure, because it appears to condone hostile manipulation of the environment with some unspecified 'benign' means. To be effective, the constraints on hostile uses of environmental forces must be unambiguously comprehensive. Such comprehensiveness could be achieved by removing the threshold established by the Convention, which limits the ban to only those uses having 'widespread, long-lasting or severe' effects. The Convention would thereby be made applicable to *any* hostile use of the modification techniques. Indeed, the very notion of a threshold of damage or injury, below which the parties retain freedom of action, seems incongruous in an agreement ostensibly banning the use of a specific method of warfare and establishing a humanitarian law of war.

It would be desirable to prohibit the hostile use of modification techniques against any state or people, instead of confining the ban – as the Environmental Modification Convention of 1977 does – to injuries to parties. It would be difficult, if not impossible, to circumscribe the effects of the use of an environmental modification technique within definite geographic boundaries so as to injure a non-party without at the same time injuring a party. An environmental weapon would also strike both combatants and noncombatants in an indiscriminate way, in contravention of the basic rule of international law requiring protection of the civilian population.

The changes to the Environmental Modification Convention of 1977 suggested above could be brought about through an amendment procedure envisaged in the Convention. Proposals for amendments may be submitted to the depositary (the United Nations Secretary-General) by any party; they may also be considered at conferences periodically convened to review the operation of the Convention and to examine the effectiveness of its provisions in eliminating the dangers of any hostile use of environmental modification techniques.

Inhumane Weapon Convention of 1980

The Inhumane Weapon Convention of 1980 provides for a mechanism to expand the area of restrictions or prohibitions on the use of weapons. Special conferences may be convened to consider amendments, as well as proposals for additional protocols relating to categories of conventional weapons not covered by the existing protocols. In addition, after a period of ten years following entry into force of the Convention, the United Nations Secretary-General (the depositary) may call a conference for the purpose of reviewing the scope and operation of the Convention and its Protocols. The Convention became effective in 1983, so that the first opportunity for such a review will arise in 1993.

It should be borne in mind that it is often easier to ban arms which are at the research and experimentation stage than to eliminate those already developed, manufactured, and stockpiled. Therefore, it would seem advisable, prior to the convening of an amendment or review conference, to hold one or more meetings of experts in order to determine whether new means of warfare developed on the basis of recent scientific discoveries could cause serious, irreparable damage to the environment in the broadest sense of the term. Such means of warfare would fall under the category of inhumane weapon and would thereby affect the humanitarian law of armed conflict. Some suggestions for strengthening the Inhumane Weapon Convention that have particular relevance to environmental protection are presented below.

Existing restrictions on the use of mines are incomplete. More specifically, Protocol II of the Inhumane Weapon Convention of 1980 does not apply to the use of anti-ship mines, either at sea or in inland waterways. In this field, the rules which were adopted as a result of Hague Convention VIII of 1907 Relative to the Laying of Automatic Submarine Contact Mines (Goldblat, 1982a, pp. 126–127; Westing, 1985, pp. 107–110) continue to be the only ones valid. But these rules are of limited value and should be updated so as to provide increased protection for peaceful shipping. Moreover, the scope of restrictions on the use of sea mines must be widened to include mines relying on magnetic, acoustic, or pressure effects or on a combination thereof.

It is essential that every sea mine be fitted with a device capable of rendering the mine harmless on command once it ceases to serve a military purpose. The location and technical characteristics of the sea mines should be carefully recorded, in accordance with generally accepted international rules, to facilitate subsequent clearance operations. It would also seem advisable to establish a standing international mechanism, preferably within the framework of the United Nations Environment Programme (Nairobi), which could be called upon to render services in the removal of unexploded land mines and sea mines, as well as of other explosive remnants of war (Westing, 1985).

Restrictions on the use in war of incendiary weapons are patently insufficient. A general prohibition similar to the ban on the use of chemical and biological weapons, still remains to be negotiated. In the meantime, some serious deficiencies in Protocol III of the Inhumane Weapon Convention of 1980 could be removed by rendering the protection of civilians more complete and by prohibiting the use of at least the most 'inhumane' incendiary weapons, such as napalm, against combatants.

It would be highly desirable to restrict the use of fuel/air explosives. These are munitions which rely for their effect on blast (shock) waves caused by the detonation of a cloud created by an inflammable substance dispersed in the air. Fuel/air explosive weapons had been designed chiefly for the clearance of mine fields, but in recent years mines have been developed which are resistant to detonation by this means. Nevertheless, there is an increased interest in using fuel/air explosive weapons for antipersonnel purposes, for example, against sheltered troops. Fuel/air explosive munitions have a major environmental impact within their area of effectiveness, killing wildlife and severely damaging the vegetation. Moreover, the wide coverage of their destructive impact threatens the release of dangerous forces, when employed in industrialized areas.

Death from blast injuries affecting the lungs is exceedingly painful. Other weapons, such as bombs, artillery shells, or grenades, also produce blast effects, but they rely chiefly on fragmentation effects. It can therefore be argued that the use of fuel/air explosive weapons, which are unique in killing exclusively by blast, contradicts the principle established by the St Petersburg Declaration of 1868 referred to above, that states should abstain from 'the employment of arms which uselessly aggravate the sufferings of disabled men, or render their death inevitable' (Goldblat, 1982a, p. 120).

V Conclusion

To date, only the *use* of certain weapons is formally regulated by special treaties. The use in war of chemical and biological weapons has long been prohibited (Goldblat, 1982a, pp. 135–136). Bans or restrictions on the use of nuclear weapons are dealt with in conjunction with prohibitions on their deployment in certain geographic areas, or with the prevention of their proliferation (Goldblat, 1982a, pp. 24–89). However, in the light of international law, even in the absence of specific legal norms, the legality of the use of nuclear weapons is open to question, as such weapons obviously fall under the category of arms which are excessively injurious or have indiscriminate effects.

The danger that the weapons prohibited for use may be resorted to under certain conditions – as has occurred on several occasions – will not disappear as long as these weapons remain in the arsenals of states. It is thus important that the very *possession* of certain weapons be proscribed. The régimes of non-use and of non-possession of weapons are mutually supportive, and it is only natural that the former régime should precede the latter: hence the intrinsic link between the development of the humanitarian law of armed conflict and progress in the field of disarmament.

With specific reference to the release of dangerous forces, it becomes crucial that rigorous attention be paid not only to specific weapons, but as well to the means of their employment and to the selection of targets.

Finally, the law of armed conflict suffers from an important weakness: the code of conduct established for belligerents in time of peace might not resist the pressure of military expedience generated in the course of hostilities. Attempts to 'humanize' war might thus prove futile. Notwithstanding this weakness, humanitarian laws are indispensable, because they corroborate the precedence of humanitarian imperatives over military considerations. It has long been recognized that even in cases not covered by international agreements, civilians and combatants 'remain under the protection and the rule of the principles of the law of nations, as they result from the usages established among civilized peoples, from the laws of humanity, and the dictates of the public conscience' (to quote the so-called Martens clause in the preamble to Hague Convention IV of 1907 [Goldblat, 1982a, p. 122]). All these legal norms and principles are binding not only upon states as such but also upon individuals and, in particular, upon the members of the armed forces. Their negation would be incompatible with the demands of human civilization.

References

Bothe, M., Partsch, K.J., & Solf, W.A. 1982. *New rules for victims of armed conflicts.* Hague: Martinus Nijhoff, 746 pp.

Bring, O. 1987. Regulating conventional weapons in the future: humanitarian law or arms control? *Journal of Peace Research*, Oslo, 24:275–286.

Goldblat, J. 1982a. *Agreements for arms control: a critical survey*. London: Taylor & Francis, 387 pp.

Goldblat, J. 1982b. Laws of armed conflict: an overview of the restrictions and limitations on the methods and means of warfare. *Bulletin of Peace Proposals*, Oslo, 13:127–133.

Goldblat, J. 1983. Convention on 'inhumane' weapons. *Bulletin of the Atomic Scientists*, Chicago, 39(1):24–25.

Goldblat, J. 1985. Explosive remnants of war: legal aspects. In: Westing, A.H. (ed.). *Explosive remnants of war: mitigating the environmental effects*. London: Taylor & Francis, 141 pp.: pp. 77–83.

Sandoz, Y., Swinarski, C., & Zimmermann, B. (eds). 1987. *Commentary on the Additional Protocols of 8 June 1977 to the Geneva Conventions of 12 August 1949*. Geneva: International Committee of the Red Cross, 1625 pp.

Sims, N. 1981. Prohibition of inhumane and indiscriminate weapons. *SIPRI Yearbook*, London, 1981:445–467.

UNGA. 1969. *Question of chemical and bacteriological (biological) weapons*. New York: UN General Assembly Resolution No. 2603A(XXIV) of 16 Dec 69, 2 pp.

Westing, A.H. 1976. *Ecological consequences of the Second Indochina War*. Stockholm: Almqvist & Wiksell, 119 pp. + 8 plates.

Westing, A.H. (ed.). 1985. *Explosive remnants of war: mitigating the environmental effects*. London: Taylor & Francis, 141 pp. [a UNEP book]

Westing, A.H. 1989. Herbicides in warfare: the case of Indochina. In: Bourdeau, P., et al. (eds). *Ecotoxicology and climate: with special reference to hot and cold climates*. Chichester, UK: John Wiley, 392 pp.: pp. 337–357.

6

Towards Preventing the Release of Dangerous Forces

Arthur H. Westing
International Peace Research Institute Oslo

I Introduction

The genocidal and ecocidal possibilities of a future nuclear war are now very widely recognized (Westing, 1987). However, less widely recognized are the potentials for human and environmental catastrophe that are becoming an ever more likely concomitant of non-nuclear war. The threat of catastrophe from non-nuclear war derives in part from the possibility that such a war might escalate to a nuclear one, but especially because of its own growing potential for devastation – in a global biosphere that is already being stretched to its very limits and beyond.

As is explained in the opening chapter, the intrinsic dangers of a non-nuclear war derive in some measure from the growing potency of conventional weapons and the means of their employment, but for the most part the dangers derive from the ever greater number of possibilities for the release of dangerous forces from the artifacts of industrialization (see Chapter 1).

Thus, the very survival of humankind now hinges upon the widespread development in all segments of society of attitudes sufficiently supportive of restrictions on the pursuit of war. This development must be able: (a) to induce the relevant governments to adopt such restraints formally, thereby developing ever more appropriate legal norms (Westing, 1989b; 1989c; 1990b); and (b) to provide the societal support that would ensure they be honored, thereby establishing ever more appropriate cultural norms (Westing, 1988b).

The present book clearly demonstrates the increasing potential for the indirect (collateral) impacts of war. Dwelt upon in the early chapters are expanding possibilities for the release of dangerous forces from nuclear power stations (see Chapter 2), from chemical plants (see Chapter 3), and from hydrological facilities (see Chapter 4). As a result, this final chapter is devoted to means of preventing such releases. First considered are technical approaches, then legal approaches, and finally cultural approaches. The question of actually eliminating interstate war itself is raised as a component of the cultural approaches, for the purpose of rendering moot the very question of wartime devastation, whether direct or indirect.

II Technical Approaches

Technical approaches to preventing the release of dangerous forces from the artifacts of an industrializing society, or of mitigating their impact, can take one or another of several forms. Thus, a potentially dangerous facility could be made more nearly safe: (a) by reconstructing the facility so that its basic design becomes more nearly inherently safe, or, in the case of a facility not yet constructed, to adopt or develop such a design; (b) by adding safety features to the facility of a more superficial nature, both physical and procedural; (c) by surrounding the facility with a buffer zone that is at least free of permanent human habitation, one large enough so that any dangerous releases would essentially spend themselves within that zone; or (d) by scrapping the facility and either substituting for it a more benign source of the societal benefits it had been providing, or else doing without.

Safer Designs and Protocols
Various possibilities exist with respect to more nearly safe design features for facilities containing potentially dangerous forces. For example, all present and any future nuclear power plants should be fitted out with massive nuclear containment structures. The core-cooling systems, both the routine ones and the emergency ones, should be rigorously protected against possible disruption, whether such disruption is on-site or off-site. And, for any future plants, the type of reactor should be chosen or designed with inherent safety as a paramount goal. As Krass points out, gas-cooled reactors (such as those prevalent in the United Kingdom) are inherently less likely to permit catastrophic releases of radioactive contaminants into the human environment than the far more widely employed water-cooled reactors, or than the graphite-cooled reactors (such as the one at Chernobyl) (see Chapter 2). Chemical plants that contain potentially dangerous forces might well be constructed partly underground and with adequate containment structures. Dams that impound large bodies of water should be built more massively than present design criteria call for. Moreover, Bergström points out that earthen dams are less subject to catastrophic failure than concrete arch dams, a matter that must therefore be considered in planning future dam constructions (see Chapter 4).

As to prudent protocols, Krass points out that wartime contingency plans for nuclear power plants subject to attack could include operation at lower power levels in order to reduce their radioactive inventory, followed by their being shut down (see Chapter 2). Similarly, Bergström suggests that wartime contingency plans for water impoundments subject to attack should include reduction of their water levels (see Chapter 4). Bergström makes the further interesting observation that if a hostile action has as its objective the disruption of an electrical supply system, then this could be accomplished more readily by attacking elements of the system other than dams, and at the same time with less of an impact on the human environment.

Buffer Zones
The establishment of buffer zones free of permanent human habitation around facilities that contain potentially dangerous forces appears to be an obvious precaution to adopt. Thus, each nuclear power plant or cluster of power plants in the human environment – of which there now exist somewhat over 200, scattered about in 26 nations – should *invariably* be surrounded by a buffer zone that would approximate the area in which rapid and long-term evacuation would be necessary, that is, an area perhaps 500 000 hectares in extent (an area having a radius of about 40 kilometers) (Westing, 1989d). The zone has to be free (or made free) of all permanent habitation, of all major transportation arteries, and of all militarily attractive targets. Moreover, it would be appropriate not to construct a nuclear plant closer than about 50 kilometers from a national frontier. Buffer zones surrounding potentially dangerous chemical plants (smaller than those just suggested for nuclear facilities) make equally good sense, as would buffer zones in areas subject to catastrophic flooding following the breaching of a dam.

Needless to say, had a buffer zone of the sort being suggested here been in place around Chernobyl, most of the immediate human agony, long-term human sequelae (psychological, somatic, teratogenic, mutagenic, genetic), and monumental post-accident expenses would have been avoided (Westing, 1989d). Indeed, the various examples of peacetime accidents involving nuclear power stations described by Krass (see Chapter 2), those involving chemical plants described by Matousek (see Chapter 3; see also Chapter 1), and those involving dams described by Bergström (see Chapter 4), combine to emphasize the enormous importance of such buffer zones in association with all artifacts in the human environment that contain dangerous forces, no matter whether releases from them might occur in time of war or peace.

Although the buffer zones being proposed here could well be devoted to agriculture, range management, or forestry, in many cases it might be even more desirable to set them aside as a nature reserve, that is, as a reserve conforming to one or another of protection categories I to V of the International Union for Conservation of Nature & Natural Resources (Gland, Switzerland) (IUCN, 1985, pp. 4–11). If the buffer zone became a nature reserve, it would add to the currently inadequate global extent of protected nature (Westing, 1990a).

Efficiency and Frugality

The possibility for release of dangerous forces can obviously be lessened by reducing the number of potentially dangerous facilities. For example, the need for electrical generating stations, whether based on nuclear energy or impounded water, could be reduced if a society were to use its energy more efficiently or more frugally.

III Legal Approaches

A body of international law does exist that has as its purpose the prevention of utter human and environmental devastation in time of war (Bring, 1987; Detter de Lupis, 1987, Part II; Goldblat, 1982; Sims, 1981; see also Chapter 5). However, it is flawed in a number of funda-mental respects: (a) the use of nuclear weapons is not thereby expressly proscribed (Westing, 1989c); (b) there is no widely accepted form of unconditional compulsory arbitration or adjudication to provide for the non-violent resolution of interstate conflict (Westing, 1990b); (c) the notion of national sovereignty remains as sacrosanct as ever; and (d) the treaties themselves are characterized by a number of weaknesses (see Chapter 5).

The noted shortcomings notwithstanding, it will be useful to sum-marize the several most salient restrictions on environmental abuse in time of war that have become embodied in international law. Such a listing is meant to fulfill two purposes: (a) to enhance the visibility of the existing legal norms, thereby helping to translate them more widely into cultural (including military) norms; and (b) to permit a recognition of both their omissions and weaknesses (even without a consideration of the numerous unilaterally attached reservations).

To begin with, there is a limited series of relevant treaties that has received rather extensive formal support. Through Hague Convention II of 1899 (and reaffirmed in Hague Convention IV of 1907, and again in Bern Protocol I of 1977), a conceptual basis for martial restraint has been established, at least to the extent that 'The right of belligerents to adopt means of injuring the enemy is not unlimited' (see Appendices 3.1, 3.2, & 3.5).

Then there are certain restrictions on specific weapons or means of war. First, the Geneva Protocol of 1925 forbids the use in war of chemical and bacteriological weapons, some of which could be environmentally devastating (Westing, 1985; 1989b); and, reinforcing this restraint, the Bacteriological and Toxin Weapon Convention of 1972 forbids the very possession of bacteriological and one class of chemical (toxin) weapons (Westing, 1988a; 1988d). Second, the Environmental Modification Convention of 1977 restricts the manipulation of the forces of nature (e.g., the action of winds or of waves) for hostile purposes (Westing, 1984; see also Appendix 3.4). In another approach to the subject, certain geographical areas are protected. Thus, the Antarctic Treaty of 1959 requires that that continent be used for peaceful purposes only (Westing, 1986, pp. 217–224).

Two closely related treaties of great relevance to the human environment in time of war are in force, Bern Protocols I and II of 1977 additional to the Geneva Conventions of 1949 (see Appendices 3.5 & 3.6). However, they have not as yet achieved the wide formal acceptance that they merit. This is a pity inasmuch as the two Protocols are especially important in the present context because they specifically address the release of dangerous forces, albeit in a rather circumscribed manner.

According to both Protocols I and II of 1977, belligerents are prohibited from attacking dams or dikes and nuclear electrical generating stations, if such actions could cause the release of dangerous forces that would cause severe losses among the civilian population (see Appendices 3.5 & 3.6).

It should be pointed out that both Protocols I and II of 1977 prohibit belligerents from rendering unavailable any objects which are indispensable to the survival of the civilian population, including foodstuffs, agricultural areas, livestock, and drinking water installations – a notion extended to times of military occupation by the principle of usufructory use previously established by Hague Convention II of 1899 and Hague Convention IV of 1907 (see Appendices 3.1 & 3.2). Moreover, as a result of Protocol I of 1977, it is even prohibited to employ means of warfare that would cause severe damage to the natural environment – a concept that receives minor reinforcement from the Inhumane Weapon Convention of 1980 (see Appendix 3.7).

The matter of eliminating interstate war itself as a means of protecting the human environment is also a question of international law, but so clearly requires changes in societal norms that it is discussed in the following section rather than in this one.

The general plea must be made that all of the nations of the world embrace the several treaties just outlined, as a contribution to minimizing wartime damage to the human environment. And to be coupled to this plea is, of course, the corollary one that each nation enact as well concomitant domestic enabling legislation. Moreover, Goldblat catalogues various shortcomings in the relevant treaties and recommends a number of possible remedies (see Chapter 5).

Focusing more narrowly on legal approaches to protecting the human environment from the release of dangerous forces in time of war, it becomes necessary to urge the many still recalcitrant countries – indeed, roughly half the nations of the world – to become party to Bern Protocols I and II of 1977 (see Appendices 3.5 & 3.6). Also relevant here is the regrettably still nascent principle that nations have the responsibility to ensure that their activities do not cause damage to the human environment in areas beyond their jurisdiction. This notion does gain modest strength from the widely adhered to Partial Test Ban Treaty of 1963, which prohibits some forms of trans-boundary radioactive air pollution (Westing, 1988d). Further modest support derives from the also widely adopted World Heritage Convention of 1972, via which it is agreed not to damage, directly or indirectly, the natural heritage situated on the territory of other nations (see Appendix 3.3). However, the notion has been most clearly enunciated in the albeit non-binding Declaration of 1972 on the Human Environment (see Appendix 4.1, Principle XXI). Needed now is a multilateral treaty that enshrines the concept and makes it generally applicable to the trans-boundary release of dangerous forces in both peacetime and wartime.

IV Cultural Approaches

Military and civil assaults on both humans and nature have, of course, been part and parcel of the human heritage for thousands of years – for as far back as the past can be reconstructed on the basis of either recorded history or archeology. Such actions have thus been condoned, if not actively supported, by humankind through countless generations. But, as suggested above, it has only been for a very few generations that such actions have become an actual threat to continued human existence. It thus seems clear that the maintenance of this planet in a condition conducive to the well-being of both present and future generations will require unprecedented constraints on traditional human actions, these in turn requiring revisions in deeply ingrained attitudes and approaches to society as well as to nature.

In order for the now undeniably necessary human constraints to be adhered to with any degree of reliability, it will be necessary for nations, *inter alia*, to take the legal steps outlined in the prior section. Multilateral treaties are of particular importance because the dangers that loom so large – both the military and the civil ones – are in most instances international in their scope. Many of those dangers have regional dimensions and some even global ones. Their mitigation thus requires cooperative action of similar scope. But in order for the needed legal instruments, whether national or international, to be enacted in the first instance, and to be respected as legal norms in the second, there is a necessity for widespread public support. It thus becomes clear that public opinion must be suitably converted and mobilized as a precursor to the development of appropriate cultural norms (Westing, 1988e).

Two key questions arise: (a) whether it will indeed be possible to develop the cultural norms recognized as being necessary; and (b) what the specific directions are that society must take within the framework of the new cultural norms.

Will New Norms Develop?
Regarding the first of the questions posed above – whether it will be possible to develop new cultural norms – the prognosis is, in fact, one of cautious optimism (Westing, 1988e). Both temporal and spatial evidence could be marshalled to demonstrate that the relevant cultural norms of *Homo sapiens* are, indeed, mutable. The human propensity for settling interstate disputes by violent means appears to derive sufficiently from societal factors for it to be amenable to change; and the human propensity for misusing the environment appears to derive sufficiently from ignorance for it to be similarly amenable to change.

The potential role of the mass media (particularly, of a truly free press) and the great importance of education, both formal and informal, are recognized as key facilitators in the process of necessary change. The activities of both professional and lay citizen groups are also seen to have an important role in the process. Moreover, it is especially interesting to note how influential individuals can be in establishing and reinforcing cultural norms, especially via creative outputs in literature, poetry, drama, and art.

One of the most heartening signs of hope for the future emanates from the countries of eastern Europe. Recent events there (especially those that have been gaining momentum since 1988) have shown the world how quickly and wholeheartedly nations, both large and small, can accept the necessity for openness and change. In that regard, it has been especially interesting to see the key role that is being played in this process by environmental groups ('green' movements). These environmental groups have been striving with imagination, forcefulness, and flair in an attempt to achieve true comprehensive human security – an agenda that includes, as it must, sincere attempts at arms reductions, at social justice, and at ecological balance.

What Must Occur?
Regarding the second of the questions posed above – the specific directions society must take within the framework of the new cultural norms – involved are such truly formidable tasks for the safeguarding of civilization as means for controlling human population growth, for limiting the numbers of domestic animals, for utilizing the world's renewable natural resources on a sustained-yield basis, for disposing of civilization's waste products (solid, liquid, and gaseous) on a

sustained-discard basis (whether this be into air, water, or soil), and for strict habitat protection in some areas (Westing, 1990a). Means for international trust and cooperation must be reinforced. And last, but by no means least, means of non-violent conflict resolution must be accepted, via the submission by all nations to compulsory arbitration of their international disputes, using the good offices of the International Court of Justice, the Permanent Court of Arbitration, or similar body (see below).

Thus in the final analysis, clearly the most important new cultural norm for humankind to embrace will have to be a deep recognition that true human security can flow only from a combination of social and environmental security (Westing, 1989a). Fortunately, as suggested earlier, there are signs that this new ethos is, in fact, beginning to take hold (see also Boulding, 1983; Ray, 1989).

Towards the Elimination of Interstate War Itself
The potential for wartime devastation, both direct and indirect, having attained the level it has, it may no longer be too far-fetched to consider seriously the possibility of fostering the spread of a cultural norm or ethos in support of eliminating interstate war itself from the human agenda (Westing, 1990b).

One of the great milestones in human history occurred in 1928 when a large number of sovereign nations, meeting in Paris, agreed that the time had finally come for a frank renunciation of war. Indeed, within a year more than 50 nations, including all of the major powers, had formally endorsed what came to be known as the Pact of Paris.[1] In so doing, the contracting parties solemnly declared that they would (Goldblat, 1982, pp. 136–137): '...condemn recourse to war for the solution of international controversies, and renounce it as an instrument of national policy in their relations with one another [and, moreover, that] the settlement or solution of all disputes or conflicts of whatever nature or of whatever origin they may be, which may arise among them, shall never be sought except by pacific means.'

For the nations of the world to join in an endeavor as humane and civilizing as the Pact of Paris of 1928 was a most extraordinary event, for until that time warfare had been widely accepted as an appropriate means of interaction between sovereign nations (or their earlier equivalents) for as long as the human past can be reconstructed

---

[1] The Pact of Paris – the Treaty providing for the Renunciation of War as an Instrument of National Policy – was signed in Paris on 27 August 1928 and entered into force on 24 July 1929; the depositary is the USA (Ferrell, 1952; Rifaat, 1979, pp. 64–79; Wallace, 1982). By 1934 (the last year in which a nation joined until 1971), the Pact of Paris of 1928 numbered as parties 62 of the then 75 sovereign nations of the world – i.e., 83%, an extraordinarily high proportion. The only recalcitrant nations of the time were Andorra, Argentina, Bolivia, El Salvador, Liechtenstein, Monaco, Mongolia, Nepal, Oman, San Marino, Uruguay, Vatican City, and Yemen.

(Ferrill, 1985; Roper, 1975; Wright, 1965). Indeed, there had probably never been a warless moment in all human history (nor has there been since).

In fact, it had not been until 1899 that the first serious attempt was made by the sovereign nations of the world (meeting at the Hague, both then and once again in 1907) to impose substantial restrictions on the *means* of warfare. That effort was to be followed in 1919 by the nations of the world imposing upon themselves important restrictions on the *justifications* for waging war, those via the Covenant of the League of Nations. But the Pact of Paris of 1928 to renounce war as an instrument of foreign policy was the first – and to date *only* – unambiguous formal worldwide attempt to achieve a world without war.[2]

The Pact of Paris of 1928 did not succeed in eliminating war – far from it – but what it did do, following some 8000 or more years of social acceptability, was to finally make interstate war an illegal activity, at least to its many parties. The authors of the Pact themselves hoped that it would provide social and moral guidance to the governments and peoples of the world and, in time, induce a psychological change in how they viewed war (Wright, 1953, p. 369).

It is, of course, a tragedy that, despite the Pact of Paris of 1928, preparation for war and war itself remain major preoccupations of human society. Thus today, between 2% and 3% of the global labor force – among them between 20% and 25% of all natural scientists and engineers – continue to be accounted for by the military sector of human society (Westing, 1988c, Table I); and roughly 20% of all revenues the nations of the world collect continue to be used for military purposes (ACDA, 1989, Table I). Of course, in considering these indicators of the size of the military sector of society, it must be recalled that only of the order of half is in support of various foreign policies (the remainder being devoted to domestic control).

As to interstate war itself, merely since World War II the armed forces of about 100 of the 170 currently extant sovereign nations of the world have intruded upon the territory of some other sovereign

---

[2] It is, of course, true that in 1945 49 sovereign nations, by ratifying the United Nations Charter, declared their determination to 'save succeeding generations from the scourge of war', a number that has since swelled to 157. The Charter denies to its parties a resort to wars of aggression (UN, 1945–1971, Articles II.3, II.4, LI, CVII, etc.). The Charter is unclear about wars of national liberation, but the United Nations General Assembly has subsequently resolved to condone them (UNGA, 1974, Article VII). Indeed, the Charter is sufficiently ambiguous about the meaning of its proscription of war to have generated literally hundreds of scholarly articles and scores of learned books devoted exclusively to attempts to define the limits on war that have been imposed by it (Röling, 1983). It might also be added that the United Nations General Assembly makes non-binding pronouncements from time to time that re-affirm the good intentions that had been formally agreed to via the Charter, for example, as to friendly interstate relations (UNGA, 1970) and the peaceful settlement of interstate disputes (UNGA, 1982).

nation for hostile purposes, such action occurring, on average, once every seven or eight weeks (Tillema, 1989, Table I & Appendix). These military interactions between nations continue to escalate into 'major' wars (here operationally defined as wars resulting in over 30 000 direct fatalities, and thus quite likely to be environmentally damaging) with sufficient frequency so that at least one of them is always in progress somewhere in the world (Westing, 1982; see also Eckhardt, 1989).

As common as interstate wars are, it is important to recall that they are *not* an obligate form of interstate interaction. Thus, although about 100 sovereign nations have, in fact, reinforced their foreign policies in this manner one or more times since 1945 (see above), this, of course, means that about 70 nations have *not* done so. Indeed, it is of great importance that such nations make their non-bellicose approach to international relations as visible as possible. That the peaceable nations make their benign foreign policies widely known is, as indicated earlier, important in order to establish and reinforce public attitudes, both domestically and internationally. The spread of such attitudes will, in turn, facilitate the firmer and wider establishment of non-bellicose cultural norms.

Non-militaristic cultural norms more conducive to sparing the human environment find their national expression in various tangible fashions, most notable among them: (a) the absence (or near-absence) of a military sector; (b) a neutral foreign policy (coupled with a non-threatening military sector); and (c) the unconditional acceptance in interstate disputes of the jurisdiction of an international court. Nations are free to adopt one or more of these approaches, at various levels of formality and permanence. Each warrants at least a brief exposé:

1 *Absence of a military sector:* A non-militarized status for a sovereign nation, or one that is essentially so, obviously remains more or less risky from a narrow security perspective, but is nevertheless a socially, environmentally, and morally extraordinarily enviable status or goal. In fact, about 28 nations fall into this category in at least a *de facto* sense, albeit most of them tiny in area and population.[3]

Only two sovereign nations are non-militarized in a formal sense, by

---

[3] The absence (or near absence) of a military sector for a nation has been determined on the basis of a lack (or near lack) of reported military expenditures (ACDA, 1989, Table I), reinforced by narrative accounts (CIA, 1987; Paxton, 1987–1988). By these criteria, 19 sovereign nations are at present without a military sector, and a further 9 (indicated here by parentheses) almost so: Andorra; (Antigua & Barbuda); Bahamas; (Barbados); (Belize); (Comoros); Dominica; (Gambia); Iceland; Kiribati; Liechtenstein; (Luxembourg); Maldives; (Malta); Monaco; Nauru; St Christopher & Nevis; St Lucia; St Vincent & Grenadines; San Marino; (Sao Tomé & Principe); (Seychelles); Solomon Islands; Tonga; Tuvalu; Vanuatu; Vatican City; and Western Samoa.

virtue of their national constitutions – Costa Rica and Japan – although, in fact, both support more or less potent armed forces.

The Costa Rican constitution states, with some ambivalence, that (Costa Rica, 1949, Article XII): 'The army as a permanent institution is proscribed. For vigilance and the preservation of the public order, there will be the necessary police forces. Only through continental agreement or for the national defense may military forces be organized....' In practice, Costa Rica maintains a very modest and non-threatening military sector (ACDA, 1989, Table I), a factor, moreover, that may have contributed to its regionally enviable social and environmental conditions (Høivik & Aas, 1981; Mata, 1984).

The Japanese constitution states, in no uncertain terms, that (Japan, 1946, Article IX): 'Aspiring sincerely to an international peace based on justice and order, the Japanese people forever renounce war as a sovereign right of the nation and the threat or use of force as means of settling international disputes. In order to accomplish the aim of the preceding [renunciation], land, sea, and air forces, as well as other war potential, will never be maintained. The right of belligerency of the state will not be recognized.' This highly laudable pledge, with its interesting history (McNelly, 1962), has, regrettably, come to be overlooked by Japan in practice (ACDA, 1989, Table I), at least for the time.

In addition to the two legally demilitarized nations, it might be noted here that a number of sub-national and extra-territorial domains also enjoy a demilitarized status of one sort or another.,[4]

2 *Neutrality:* A neutral status for a sovereign nation, one in which the nation establishes, or has had imposed upon it, an aloofness from the military interactions among the other nations of the world has much to say for it, especially if it has some sort of formal international status, or at least if it is built into the national constitution. Neutral nations usually consider it necessary to maintain a military sector, albeit a non-threatening one.

In fact, apparently only four neutral nations exist today for which that status enjoys formal international recognition: (a) Austria, by virtue of a parliamentary act (a 'constitutional law') of 1955, subsequently

---

[4] The sub-national and extra-territorial domains that have a legal demilitarized status of one sort or another include: (a) the Åland Islands, by virtue of the Aaland Island Convention of 1921 (Articles III, etc.) (Goldblat, 1982, pp. 133–134); (b) a number of Italian islands (Pantellaria; the Pelagian Islands, including Lampedusa; and Pianosa) plus a number of now Greek islands (the Dodecanese Islands, including Rhodes), all by virtue of the World War II Italian peace treaty (Articles XIV & IL) (Italy *et al.*, 1947); (c) the Svalbard archipelago and Bear Island, by virtue of the Spitsbergen Treaty of 1920 (Article IX) (Westing, 1986, pp. 211–216); (d) Antarctica, by virtue of the Antarctic Treaty of 1959 (Article I.1) (Westing, 1986, pp. 217–224); and (e) the moon, by virtue of the Outer Space Treaty of 1967 (Article IV) and the Moon Agreement of 1979 (Article III.1) (Westing, 1986, pp. 225–232,261–270).

recognized by a number of nations (Keesing, 1955–1956); (b) Malta, by virtue of a declaration of 1980, reinforced by a treaty with Italy in 1980, and subsequently recognized by a number of nations (Keesing, 1981; 1982); (c) Switzerland, by virtue of the Congress of Vienna of 1815, which led to the Treaty of Paris of 1815 (Articles LXXXIV & VIIIC), and by a number of subsequent reinforcements (Black et al., 1968, pp. 21–24); and (d) Vatican City, by virtue of the Lateran Treaty of 1929 (Vatican City & Italy, 1929, Article XXIV).

A number of additional nations have declared their neutrality unilaterally, but without the support of their constitutions and apparently without formal recognition by other nations (Black et al., 1968; Karsh, 1988). This group of informally and unilaterally neutral nations includes: (a) Costa Rica, since 1983 (Rhenán-Segura, 1986); (b) Finland, apparently since 1938 (Osmanczyk, 1985, p. 541); (c) Ireland, since 1939 (Keesing, 1937–1940); and (d) Sweden, perhaps since 1912 (Osmanczyk, 1985, p. 541).

3 *Submission to jurisdiction by an international court:* Probably the single most important immediate action that a sovereign nation can take as a step towards the elimination of interstate war is to submit its inevitably numerous interstate disputes to non-violent resolution by formal arbitration or adjudication. At least two important structures are already in place that serve eminently well as vehicles for such benign intercourse: (a) the Permanent Court of Arbitration, established at the Hague in 1899; and (b) the International Court of Justice (the so-called World Court), established at the Hague in 1920 as the Permanent Court of International Justice, and in its present form, within the United Nations system, in 1945.

Either of the two noted courts is in principle equally useful for the fair and impartial resolution of interstate conflicts, including environmentally based conflicts, but the International Court has a recognized mechanism by which a nation can submit to its jurisdiction (UN, 1945–1971, Statute Article XXXVI.2). It is patently clear that all of the nations of the world should submit to the compulsory and *unconditional* jurisdiction of the International Court. In fact, only about 25 nations have to date taken this crucially important step.[5]

---

[5] An only slowly growing number of sovereign nations has formally submitted to the compulsory jurisdiction of the International Court of Justice on an *unconditional* basis (or virtually so), in conformity with Article XXXVI.2 of the Court Statute. As of late 1989, 19 have done so unconditionally, and a further 6 (indicated here by parentheses) with only inconsequential reservations (ICJ, 1987–1988; updated by the depositary): (Australia since 1975); Austria since 1971; (Belgium since 1958 or earlier); Colombia since 1937; Costa Rica since 1973; Denmark since 1956 or earlier; the Dominican Republic since 1933; Finland since 1958; Haiti since 1921; (Japan since 1958); Liechtenstein since 1950; Luxembourg since 1930; Nauru since 1988; the Netherlands since 1956 or earlier; Nicaragua since 1929; Nigeria since 1965; Norway since 1976 or earlier; Panama since 1921; (Portugal since 1955); Sweden since 1957 or earlier; Switzerland since 1948; (Togo since 1979); Uganda since 1963; Uruguay since 1921; and (Zaïre since 1989).

Thus, elimination of war as an instrument of foreign policy ought to be approached in a series of actions:

1 The 59 sovereign nations of today that in the late 1920s and early 1930s formally condemned and renounced 'recourse to war for the solution of international controversies' (as embodied in the Pact of Paris of 1928) should at this time publicly reaffirm their commitment to this ideal. Equally important, the 13 nations of the time that had neglected to become parties plus the 98 nations that have appeared on the world stage since then must now also make the same formal pledge. Indeed, following a hiatus of almost four decades, a number of those nations have, in fact, been acceding to the Pact of Paris: Antigua & Barbuda, in 1988; Barbados, in 1971; Dominica, in 1988; Fiji, in 1973; and Tonga, in 1971.[6]

2 Reaffirmation or accession to the Pact of Paris of 1928 by all 170 nations should be coupled, as necessary, with constitutional amendments modelled after Article IX of the Japanese constitution (see above), in order for each sovereign nation to further reinforce the principle that 'the right of belligerency of the state will not be recognized'.

3 Of utmost importance, the 145 nations that have not as yet submitted to compulsory unconditional jurisdiction by the International Court of Justice, must do so forthwith.

4 The improved legal régimes suggested must be reinforced by a heightened public awareness of their socially and environmentally urgent necessity. As noted earlier, this required reorientation of public attitudes can best be accomplished through educational means, both formal and informal. It is, of course, necessary to nurture non-bellicose and pro-environmental cultural norms, because only with such support will there be any hope for the peaceful legal norms being stressed here to be respected.

5 As the four suggested actions just outlined become ever more widely carried out, more and more nations will presumably consider it feasible to begin a process of demilitarization – a truly major step towards eliminating war as an instrument of foreign policy, one that will make feasible the attainment of a sane policy towards the human environment.

---

[6] The Kingdom of Tonga, although not as yet officially listed as a party to the Pact of Paris of 1928, in fact acceded to it by a letter dated 22 June 1971. Tonga's letter of accession had been addressed by mistake to France as the depositary rather than to the USA (perhaps because 'Paris' appears in a commonly used name of the treaty). There the letter became buried and lost in the French government archives until serendipitously discovered by the present author in June 1989.

V Conclusion

The World Charter for Nature of 1982 proclaims that 'Nature shall be secured against degradation by warfare or other hostile activities'; and, further, that 'Special precautions shall be taken to prevent discharge [into natural systems] of radioactive or toxic wastes' (see Appendix 4.2). This mutually supporting pair of admonitions must be taken to heart by all of the peoples of the world in order to ensure for themselves and subsequent generations a habitable, fruitful, and reasonably pleasant human environment – one, moreover, that can be exploited in a manner that permits its sharing with the other creatures on earth.

As industrialization progresses and spreads ever more widely throughout the world, this book makes it amply clear that the freedom to wage war shrinks apace. The time has thus arrived when the admonitions enunciated by the World Charter for Nature must be universally recognized as obligate prerequisites for the survival and wellbeing of civilization. With the development of such understanding, the task of translating them into more formal and binding instruments will presumably become achievable.

References

ACDA. 1989. *World military expenditures and arms transfers 1988*. Washington: US Arms Control & Disarmament Agency, Publication No. 131, 137 pp.

Black, C.E., Falk, R.A., Knorr, K., & Young, O.R. 1968. *Neutralization and world politics*. Princeton, New Jersey: Princeton University Press, 195 pp.

Boulding, K. 1983. Conditions and prospects of global demilitarization: reflections on values, science, war and peace: what signs of hope? *Bulletin of Peace Proposals*, Oslo, 14:351–354.

Bring, O. 1987. Regulating conventional weapons in the future: humanitarian law or arms control? *Journal of Peace Research*, Oslo, 24:275–286.

CIA. 1987. *World factbook*. 7th ed. McLean, Virginia: US Central Intelligence Agency, 290 pp.

Costa Rica. 1949. Constitution of the Republic of Costa Rica (7 November 1949, as amended to 1963). In: Xydis, D.P. (ed.). 1968–1985. *Constitutions of nations*. 3rd-4th eds. Hague: Martinus Nijhoff, 4 volumes (1141+1810+1315+1344 pp.): Volume IV, pp. 328–362.

Detter de Lupis, I. 1987. *Law of war*. Cambridge, UK: Cambridge University Press, 411 pp.

Eckhardt, W. 1989. Civilian deaths in wartime. *Bulletin of Peace Proposals*, Oslo, 20:89–98.

Ferrell, R.H. 1952. *Peace in their time: the origins of the Kellogg–Briand pact*. New Haven: Yale University Press, 293 pp.

Ferrill, A. 1985. *Origins of war: from the Stone Age to Alexander the Great*. New York: Thames & Hudson, 240 pp.

Goldblat, J. 1982. *Agreements for arms control: a critical survey*. London: Taylor & Francis, 387 pp.

Høivik, T., & Aas, S. 1981. Demilitarization in Costa Rica: a farewell to arms? *Journal of Peace Research*, Oslo, 18:333–351.

ICJ. 1987–1988. Declarations recognizing as compulsory the jurisdiction of the Court. *International Court of Justice Yearbook*, Hague, 42:62–97.

Italy *et al.* 1947. Treaty of peace with Italy (10 February 1947). In: Leiss, A.C. (ed.). 1954. *European peace treaties after World War II: negotiations and texts of treaties with Italy, Bulgaria, Hungary, Rumania, and Finland.* Boston: World Peace Foundation, 341 pp.: pp. 163–250.

IUCN. 1985. *1985 United Nations list of national parks and protected areas.* 3rd ed. Gland, Switz.: International Union for Conservation of Nature & Natural Resources, 174 pp.

Japan. 1946. Constitution of Japan (3 November 1946). In: Xydis, D.P. (ed.). 1968–1985. *Constitutions of nations.* 3rd-4th eds. Hague: Martinus Nijhoff, 4 volumes (1141+1810+1315+1344 pp.): Volume II, pp. 414–425.

Karsh, E. 1988. International co-operation and neutrality. *Journal of Peace Research,* Oslo, 25:57–67.

Keesing. 1937–1940. Eire. *Keesing's Contemporary Archives,* London, 3:3531.

Keesing. 1955–1956. Austria. *Keesing's Contemporary Archives,* London, 10:14561, 14570, 14602.

Keesing. 1981. Malta. *Keesing's Contemporary Archives,* London, 27:30710–30711.

Keesing. 1982. Malta. *Keesing's Contemporary Archives,* London, 28:31339–31340.

Mata, L. 1984. Investing in education and health versus militarism: the case of Costa Rica. *IPPNW [International Physicians for the Prevention of Nuclear War] Report,* Boston, 2(3):22–25.

McNelly, T. 1962. Renunciation of war in the Japanese constitution. *Political Science Quarterly,* New York, 77:350–378.

Osmanczyk, E.J. 1985. *Encyclopedia of the United Nations and international agreements.* London: Taylor & Francis, 1059 pp.

Paxton, J. (ed.). 1987–1988. *Statesman's year-book.* 124th ed. London: Macmillan, 1695 pp.

Ray, J.L. 1989. Abolition of slavery and the end of international war. *International Organization,* Stanford, 43:405–439.

Rhenán-Segura, J. 1986. Costa Rica: neutrality. In: Laszlo, E., & Yoo, J.Y. (eds). *World encyclopedia of peace.* Oxford: Pergamon, 4 volumes (639+596+363+294 pp.): Volume I, pp. 205–206.

Rifaat, A.M. 1979. *International aggression: a study of the legal concept: its development and definition in international law.* Stockholm: Almqvist & Wiksell, 355 pp.

Röling, B.V.A. 1983. On the prohibition of the use of force. In: Blackshield, A.R. (ed.). *Legal change: essays in honour of Julius Stone.* Sydney: Butterworths, 367 pp.: pp. 274–298.

Roper, M.K. 1975. Evidence of warfare in the Near East from 10,000–4,300 B.C. In: Nettleship, M.A., *et al.* (eds). *War, its causes and correlates.* Hague: Mouton, 813 pp.: pp. 299–343.

Sims, N. 1981. Prohibition of inhumane and indiscriminate weapons. *SIPRI Yearbook,* London, 1981:445–467.

Tillema, H.K. 1989. Foreign overt military intervention in the nuclear age. *Journal of Peace Research,* Oslo, 26:179–196,419–420.

UN. 1945–1971. *Charter of the United Nations and Statute of the International Court of Justice.* New York: United Nations. [Reprinted in: *UN Yearbook,* New York, 38:1297–1310; 1984.]

UNGA. 1970. *Declaration on principles of international law concerning friendly relations and co-operation among states in accordance with the Charter of the United Nations.* New York: UN General Assembly, Resolution No. 2625(XXV) (24 Oct 70). [Reprinted in: *UN Yearbook,* New York, 24:788–792; 1970.]

UNGA. 1974. *Definition of aggression.* New York: UN General Assembly, Resolution No. 3314(XXIX) (14 Dec 74). [Reprinted in: *UN Yearbook,* New York, 28:846–848; 1974.]

UNGA. 1982. *Manila declaration on the peaceful settlement of international disputes.* New York: UN General Assembly, Resolution No. 37/10 (15 Nov 82). [Reprinted in: *UN Yearbook*, New York, 36:1372–1374; 1982.]

Vatican City & Italy. 1929. Lateran treaty (11 February 1929). In: Xydis, D.P. (ed.). 1968–1985. *Constitutions of nations.* 3rd-4th eds. Hague: Martinus Nijhoff, 4 volumes (1141+1810+1315+1344 pp.): Volume III, pp. 1187–1194.

Wallace, C.D. 1982. Kellogg–Briand Pact (1928). In: Bernhardt, R. (ed.). *Encyclopedia of public international law. III. Use of force; war and neutrality; peace treaties (A–M).* Amsterdam: North-Holland Publishing, 299 pp.: pp. 236–239.

Westing, A.H. 1982. War as a human endeavor: the high-fatality wars of the twentieth century. *Journal of Peace Research*, Oslo, 19:261–270.

Westing, A.H. 1984. Environmental warfare: an overview. In: Westing, A.H. (ed.). *Environmental warfare: a technical, legal and policy appraisal.* London: Taylor & Francis, 107 pp.: pp. 3–12. [a UNEP book]

Westing, A.H. 1985. Towards eliminating the scourge of chemical war: reflections on the occasion of the sixtieth anniversary of the Geneva Protocol. *Bulletin of Peace Proposals*, Oslo, 16:117–120.

Westing, A.H. (ed.). 1986. *Global resources and international conflict: environmental factors in strategic policy and action.* Oxford: Oxford University Press, 280 pp. [a UNEP book]

Westing, A.H. 1987. Ecological dimension of nuclear war. *Environmental Conservation*, Geneva, 14:295–306.

Westing, A.H. 1988a. Cultural constraints on warfare: micro-organisms as weapons. *Medicine & War*, London, 4:85–95.

Westing, A.H. (ed.). 1988b. *Cultural norms, war and the environment.* Oxford: Oxford University Press, 177 pp. [a UNEP book]

Westing, A.H. 1988c. Military sector *vis-à-vis* the environment. *Journal of Peace Research*, Oslo, 25:257–264.

Westing, A.H. 1988d. Multilateral treaties constraining military disruption of the environment: excerpts. In: Westing, A.H. (ed.). *Cultural norms, war and the environment.* Oxford: Oxford University Press, 177 pp.: pp. 163–168.

Westing, A.H. 1988e. Towards non-violent conflict resolution and environmental protection: a synthesis. In: Westing, A.H. (ed.). *Cultural norms, war and the environment.* Oxford: Oxford University Press, 177 pp.: pp. 151–159. [A UNEP book]

Westing, A.H. 1989a. Comprehensive human security and ecological realities. *Environmental Conservation*, Geneva, 16: 295.

Westing, A.H. 1989b. Geneva Protocol of 1925: towards a full renunciation of chemical warfare. *Transnational Perspectives*, Geneva, 15(2):21–22.

Westing, A.H. 1989c. Proposal for an international treaty for protection against nuclear devastation. *Bulletin of Peace Proposals*, Oslo, 20:435–436.

Westing, A.H. 1989d. Reflections on the occasion of the third anniversary of the Chernobyl disaster. *Environmental Conservation*, Geneva, 16:100–101.

Westing, A.H. 1990a. Our place in nature: reflections on the global carrying-capacity for humans. In: Polunin, N., & Burnett, J.H. (eds). *Maintenance of the biosphere.* Edinburgh: Edinburgh University Press, 228 pp.: pp. 109–120.

Westing, A.H. 1990b. Towards eliminating war as an instrument of foreign policy. *Bulletin of Peace Proposals*, Oslo, 21:29–35.

Wright, Q. 1953. Outlawry of war and the law of war. *American Journal of International Law*, Washington, 47:365–376.

Wright, Q. 1965. *Study of war: with a commentary on war since 1942.* 2nd ed. Chicago: University of Chicago Press, 1637 pp. + tables.

Appendix 1
Environmental Hazards of War in an Industrializing World: Select Bibliography

Anspaugh, L.R., Catlin, R.J., & Goldman, M. 1988. Global impact of the Chernobyl reactor accident. *Science*, Washington, 242: 1513–1519.

Berg, P., & Herolf, G. 1984. 'Deep strike': new technologies for conventional interdiction. *SIPRI Yearbook*, London, 1984:291–318.

Björnerstedt, R., *et al.* 1973. *Napalm and other incendiary weapons and all aspects of their possible use.* New York: United Nations, 63 pp. [Also: Document No. A/8803/Rev.1.]

Blix, H. 1978. Area bombardment: rules and reasons. *British Year Book of International Law*, Oxford, 49:31–69.

Bonaccorsi, A., Fanelli, R., & Tognoni, G. 1978. In the wake of Seveso. *Ambio*, Stockholm, 7:234–239.

Bowonder, B., Kasperson, J.X., & Kasperson, R.E. 1985. Avoiding future Bhopals. *Environment*, Washington, 27(7):6–13,31–37.

Brickhill, P. 1951. *Dam busters.* London: Evans Brothers, 269 pp. + 13 plates.

Bring, O. 1987. Regulating conventional weapons in the future: humanitarian law or arms control? *Journal of Peace Research*, Oslo, 24:275–286.

Davis, L.N. 1979. *Frozen fire: where will it happen next?* San Francisco: Friends of the Earth, 298 pp.

Detter de Lupis, I. 1987. *Law of war.* Cambridge, UK: Cambridge University Press, 411 pp.

Dupuy, T.N. 1978–1979. Weapons lethality and the nuclear threshold. *Armed Forces Journal International*, Washington, 116(2):24, 26–27,33.

Fay, J.A., & MacKenzie, J.J. 1972. Cold cargo. *Environment*, Washington, 14(9):21–22,27–29.

Fetter, S.A., & Tsipis, K. 1981. Catastrophic releases of radioactivity. *Scientific American*, New York, 244(4):33–39,146.

Goldblat, J. 1982. Laws of armed conflict: an overview of the restrictions and limitations on the methods and means of warfare. *Bulletin of Peace Proposals*, Oslo, 13:127–133.

Goldblat, J. 1983. Convention on 'inhumane' weapons. *Bulletin of the Atomic Scientists*, Chicago, 39(1):24–25.

Heinisch, E., Kläss, V., & Klein, S. 1989. *Kriegsuntauglichkeit moderner Industriegesellschaften Beispiel Chemieindustrie: das Katastrophenpotential chemischer Industrieanlagen unter Berücksichtigung spezieller geoökologischer und ökotoxikologischer Aspekte [Incompatibility with war of modern industrial corporations, for example, the chemical industry: the potential for catastrophe of chemical industrial installations in consideration of special geo-ecological and eco-toxicological aspects]* (in German). [East] Berlin: DDR-Komitee für wissenschaftliche Fragen der Sicherung des Friedens und der Abrüstung, Informationen No. 2/1989, 55 pp.

Hewitt, K. 1983. Place annihilation: area bombing and the fate of urban places. *Annals of the Association of American Geographers*, Washington, 73:257–284.

Hippel, F.v., & Cochran, T.B. 1986. Chernobyl: the emerging story: estimating long-term health effects. *Bulletin of the Atomic Scientists*, Chicago, 43(7):18–24.

Hohenemser, C. 1988. Accident at Chernobyl: health and environmental consequences and the implications for risk management. *Annual Review of Energy*, Palo Alto, Calif., 13:383–428.

Homberger, E., Reggiani, G., Sambeth, J., & Wipf, H.K. 1979. Seveso accident: its nature, extent and consequences. *Annals of Occupational Hygiene*, Oxford, 22:327–370.

Iklé, F.C. 1958. *Social impact of bomb destruction*. Norman: University of Oklahoma Press, 250 pp. + 10 photos.

Klare, M.T. 1985. NATO's improved conventional weapons. *Technology Review*, Cambridge, Mass., 88(4):34–40,73.

Lumsden, M. 1975. 'Conventional war' and human ecology. *Ambio*, Stockholm, 4:223–228.

Lumsden, M. 1975. *Incendiary weapons*. Stockholm: Almqvist & Wiksell, 255 pp. + 12 plates.

Lumsden, M. 1978. *Anti-personnel weapons*. London: Taylor & Francis, 299 pp. + 14 plates.

MacIsaac, D. (ed.). 1976. *United States strategic bombing survey*. New York: Garland Press, 10 volumes (*ca* 3400 pp.).

Matousek, J. 1989. Impact on the social environment of a war with 'conventional' weapons. *Scientific World*, London, 33(1):14–18. [Summary in: *New Perspectives*, Helsinki, 19(4):6–7.]

Ramberg, B. 1984. *Nuclear power plants as weapons for the enemy: an unrecognized military peril*. Berkeley: University of California Press, 193 pp.

Robinson, J.P. 1979. *Effects of weapons on ecosystems*. Oxford: Pergamon Press, 70 pp. [a UNEP book]

Röling, B.V.A., & Sukovic, O. 1976. *Law of war and dubious weapons*. Stockholm: Almqvist & Wiksell, 78 pp.

Shaw, M. 1983. United Nations Convention on Prohibitions or Restrictions on the Use of Certain Conventional Weapons, 1981. *Review of International Studies*, Guildford, UK, 9:109–121.

Sims, N. 1981. Prohibition of inhumane and indiscriminate weapons. *SIPRI Yearbook*, London, 1981:445–467.

Stöhr, R. 1982. Dangerous weapons systems. *Scientific World*, London, 26(3):21–24.

Stöhr, R., & Schneider, M.M. 1988. *Flächenwirksame Waffen und Kampfmethoden für einen nichtnuklearen Landkrieg [Area weapons and methods of combat for a non-nuclear land war]* (in German). [East] Berlin: DDR-Komitee für wissenschaftliche Fragen der Sicherung des Friedens und der Abrüstung, Informationen No. 2/1988, 68 pp.

UNEP. 1980. Environmental effects of military activity. *State of the Environment*, Nairobi, 1980:35–42,51–55.

Westing, A.H. 1976. *Ecological consequences of the Second Indochina War*. Stockholm: Almqvist & Wiksell, 119 pp. + 8 plates.

Westing, A.H. 1977. *Weapons of mass destruction and the environment*. London: Taylor & Francis, 95 pp.

Westing, A.H. 1980. *Warfare in a fragile world: military impact on the human environment*. London: Taylor & Francis, 249 pp.

Westing, A.H. 1981. Environmental impact of conventional warfare. In: Barnaby, W. (ed.). *War and environment*. Stockholm: Royal Ministry of Agriculture, Environmental Advisory Council, 154 pp.: pp. 58–72.

Westing, A.H. 1984. How much damage can modern war create? In: Barnaby, F. (ed.). *Future war*. London: Michael Joseph, 192 pp.: pp. 114–124.

Westing, A.H. 1987. Ecological dimension of nuclear war. *Environmental Conservation*, Geneva, 14:295–306.

Westing, A.H., & Lumsden, M. 1979. *Threat of modern warfare to man and his environment: an annotated bibliography*. Paris: UNESCO Reports & Papers in the Social Sciences No. 40, 25 pp.

Wilson, R. 1986–1987. Chernobyl: assessing the accident. *Issues in Science & Technology*, Washington, 3(1):21–29;(2):6.

Appendix 2
Dangerous forces in
an Industrializing World

Territory	Civil nuclear reactors (No.)	Industrial chemical workers (10^3)	Large dams (No.)
Afghanistan	0	2	1
Albania	0	?	2
Angola	0	?	2
Argentina	2	14	8
Australia	0	18	32
Austria	0	22	0
Bangladesh	0	6	1
Belgium	8	71	0
Brazil	1	?	82
Bulgaria	5	35	2
Burkina Faso	0	?	1
Cambodia	0	?	1
Cameroon	0	?	3
Canada	21	35	67
Chile	0	2	5
China	0	3088	74
Colombia	0	15	7
Costa Rica	0	0	1
Cuba	0	29	1
Czechoslovakia	9	98	1
Denmark	0	12	0
Dominican Rep	0	2	2
Ecuador	0	1	1
Egypt	0	?	2
El Salvador	0	0	1
Ethiopia	0	0	2
Finland	4	14	9
France	60	125	3
German DR	5	344	0
FR Germany	29	559	0
Ghana	0	1	3
Greece	0	7	5
Guatemala	0	1	0
Honduras	0	0	2

Hungary	4	42	0
Iceland	0	0	1
India	6	187	59
Indonesia	0	23	5
Iran	0	10	8
Iraq	0	26	6
Ireland	0	12	0
Israel	0	19	0
Italy	4	211	0
Ivory Coast	0	2	3
Japan	39	190	1
Jordan	0	3	0
Kenya	0	3	1
Korea, Rep	8	38	5
Kuwait	0	2	0
Laos	0	?	1
Luxembourg	0	5	0
Madagascar	0	1	0
Malaysia	0	6	4
Mali	0	?	2
Mexico	0	30	32
Mongolia	0	2	0
Morocco	0	?	6
Mozambique	0	?	4
Netherlands	2	111	4
New Zealand	0	5	6
Nicaragua	0	2	1
Nigeria	0	1	7
Norway	0	9	8
Pakistan	1	14	3
Panama	0	0	3
Paraguay	0	?	2
Peru	0	8	1
Philippines	0	9	4
Poland	0	107	0
Portugal	0	13	3
Romania	0	210	4
Senegal	0	4	1
Singapore	0	3	0
South Africa	2	95	6
Spain	10	45	20
Sri Lanka	0	5	4
Swaziland	0	1	0
Sweden	13	18	13
Switzerland	5	67	0
Syria	0	19	0
Taiwan	6	?	1
Tanzania	0	3	1
Thailand	0	?	10
Trinidad & Tob	0	4	0
Turkey	0	28	17
United Kingdom	43	151	0
Uruguay	0	2	4
USA	119	418	>129

USSR	59	2203	55
Venezuela	0	10	10
Yugoslavia	1	58	6
Zimbabwe	0	4	2
World (170)	*466*	*>8940*	*>777*

Sources and notes: Civil nuclear reactors are those in operation (total, 429) or shut down (total, 37) as at 31 December 1988 (IAEA, 1989, Tables 1 & 13); see also Tables 2.1 & 2.2 in this book. Industrial chemical workers are those falling within International Standard Industrial Classification No. 351, the values applying primarily to 1985 (*UN Industrial Statistics Yearbook*, New York, 19(1) [1985]); the number for China includes Hong Kong (8 x 10^3), and that for the USA includes Puerto Rico (17 x 10^3). Numbers of industrial chemical *workers* are used here in the absence of adequate data on numbers of industrial chemical *plants*. Large dams are those at least 15 meters in height and impounding at least 500 million cubic meters of water (ICOLD, 1984; see also Mermel, 1988); the value for Norway is an augmented one (NWREA, 1988, p. 7); the value for the USA is too low, accounting for only those dams at least 30 meters in height. Of the 777 dams in 70 countries listed here, 255 dams in 42 countries impound 500–999 million cubic meters of water; and 522 dams in 63 countries impound 1000 million cubic meters or more of water. Appendix prepared by A.H. Westing.

References

IAEA. 1989. *Nuclear power reactors in the world.* 9th ed. Vienna: International Atomic Energy Agency, Reference Data Series No. 2, 60 pp.

ICOLD. 1984. *World register of dams.* 3rd ed. Paris: International Commission on Large Dams, 753 pp.

Mermel, T.W. 1988. Major dams of the world: 1988. *International Water Power & Dam Construction*, Sutton, UK, 40(6):52–64.

NWREA. 1988. *Energy in Norway.* Oslo: Norwegian Water Resources & Energy Administration, 10 pp.

Appendix 3
Environmental Hazards of War in an Industrializing World: Relevant Multilateral Agreements (Excerpts)[1]

Contents

---

[1] The full texts of one or more of the quoted documents are available in various works (e.g., Goldblat, 1982; Roberts & Guelff, 1982; Schindler & Toman, 1988), as are the parties to them (e.g., Ferm, 1989); or else are available from the respective depositaries.

Appendix 3.1 Convention II with Respect to the Laws and Customs of War on Land [Hague, 1899]

Depositary: The Netherlands. *Entry into force:* 1900. *States parties as of late 1989 include:* 48 of all *ca* 170 states (among them, France, the United Kingdom, the USA, and the USSR).[2]

. . .

Annex Article XXII. The right of belligerents to adopt means of injuring the enemy is not unlimited.

. . .

Annex Article LV. The occupying State shall only be regarded as administrator and usufructuary of the public buildings, real property, forests and agricultural works belonging to the hostile State, and situated in the occupied country. It must protect the capital of these properties, and administer it according to the rules of usufruct.

. . .

Appendix 3.2 Convention IV Respecting the Laws and Customs of War on Land [Hague, 1907]

Depositary: The Netherlands. *Entry into force:* 1910. *States parties as of late 1989 include:* 36 of all *ca* 170 states (among them, France, the United Kingdom, the USA, and the USSR).[3]

. . .

Annex Article XXII. The right of belligerents to adopt means of injuring the enemy is not unlimited.

. . .

Annex Article LV. The occupying State shall be regarded only as administrator and usufructuary of public buildings, real estate, forests, and agricultural estates belonging to the hostile State, and situated in the occupied country. It must safeguard the capital of these properties, and administer them in accordance with the rules of usufruct.

. . .

Appendix 3.3 World Heritage Convention [Paris, 1972]

Depositary: UNESCO. *Entry into force:* 1975. *States parties as of late 1989 include:* 106 of all *ca* 170 states (among them, China, France, the United Kingdom, the USA, and the USSR).

[2] Hague Convention II of 1899 is replaced, as applicable, by Hague Convention IV of 1907 (see its Article IV) among the parties to the latter. Thirty-one states belong to both of these conventions; 17 of the 48 parties to the former are not a party to the latter; 5 of the 36 parties to the latter are not a party to the former.
[3] Hague Convention II of 1899 is replaced, as applicable, by Hague Convention IV of 1907 (see its Article IV) among the parties to the latter. Thirty-one states belong to both of these conventions; 17 of the 48 parties to the former are not a party to the latter; 5 of the 36 parties to the latter are not a party to the former.

. . .

Article VI.1. . . . .The States Parties to this Convention recognize that [the natural] heritage[4] constitutes a world heritage for whose protection it is the duty of the international community as a whole to co-operate.

. . .

Article VI.3. Each State Party to this Convention undertakes not to take any deliberate measures which might damage directly or indirectly the . . . natural heritage . . . situated on the territory of other States Parties to this Convention.

. . .

Appendix 3.4 Environmental Modification Convention [Geneva, 1977]

Depositary: United Nations Secretary-General. *Entry into force:* 1978. *States parties as of late 1989 include:* 53 of all *ca* 170 states (among them, the United Kingdom, the USA, and the USSR).

. . .

Article I.1. Each State Party to this Convention undertakes not to engage in military or any other hostile use of environmental modification techniques[5] having widespread, long-lasting or severe effects as the means of destruction, damage or injury to any other State Party.

. . .

Appendix 3.5 Protocol I on the Protection of Victims of International Armed Conflicts [Bern, 1977][6]

Depositary: Switzerland. *Entry into force:* 1978. *States parties as of late 1989 include:* 84 of all *ca* 170 states (among them, China and the USSR).

[4] The World Heritage Convention of 1972 defines 'natural heritage' as: 'natural features consisting of physical and biological formations or groups of such formations, which are of outstanding universal value from the aesthetic or scientific point of view; geological and physiographical formations and precisely delineated areas which constitute the habitat of threatened species of animals and plants of outstanding universal value from the point of view of science or conservation; natural sites or precisely delineated natural areas of outstanding universal value from the point of view of science, conservation or natural beauty' (Article II).

It is for each State Party to this Convention to identify and delineate the different properties situated on its territory as a potential component of the world natural heritage (Article III). The States Parties select from among these the composition of the world natural heritage (Article XI.2).

[5] The Environmental Modification Convention of 1977 defines 'environmental modification techniques' as: 'any technique for changing – through the deliberate manipulation of natural processes – the dynamics, composition or structure of the earth, including its biota, lithosphere, hydrosphere and atmosphere, or of outer space' (Article II).

[6] Both Bern Protocols I and II of 1977 are additional to the Geneva Conventions of 1949 relating to Protection of Victims of Armed Conflicts.

. . .

Article XXXV.1. In any armed conflict, the right of the Parties to the conflict to choose methods or means of warfare is not unlimited.

. . .

Article XXXV.3. It is prohibited to employ methods or means of warfare which are intended, or may be expected, to cause widespread, long-term and severe damage to the natural environment. [See also Article LV.1.]

. . .

Article LIV.2. It is prohibited to attack, destroy, remove or render useless objects indispensable to the survival of the civilian population, such as foodstuffs, agricultural areas for the production of foodstuffs, crops, livestock, drinking water installations and supplies and irrigation works, for the specific purpose of denying them for their sustenance value to the civilian population or to the adverse Party, whatever the motive, whether in order to starve out civilians, to cause them to move away, or for any other motive.

. . .

Article LV.1. Care shall be taken in warfare to protect the natural environment against widespread, long-term and severe damage. This protection includes a prohibition of the use of methods or means of warfare which are intended or may be expected to cause such damage to the natural environment and thereby to prejudice the health or survival of the population. [See also Article XXXV.3.]

. . .

Article LVI.1. Works or installations containing dangerous forces, namely dams, dykes and nuclear electrical generating stations, shall not be made the object of attack, even where these objects are military objectives, if such attack may cause the release of dangerous forces and consequent severe losses among the civilian population. Other military objectives located at or in the vicinity of these works or installations shall not be made the object of attack if such attack may cause the release of dangerous forces from the works or installations and consequent severe losses among the civilian population.

. . .

Appendix 3.6 Protocol II on the Protection of Victims of Non-International Armed Conflicts [Bern, 1977][7]

Depositary: Switzerland. *Entry into force:* 1978. *States parties as of late 1989 include:* 74 of all *ca* 170 states (among them, China, France, and the USSR).

[7] Both Bern Protocols I and II of 1977 are additional to the Geneva Conventions of 1949 relating to Protection of Victims of Armed Conflicts.

. . .

Article XIV. Starvation of civilians as a method of combat is prohibited. It is therefore prohibited to attack, destroy, remove or render useless, for that purpose, objects indispensable to the survival of the civilian population, such as foodstuffs, agricultural areas for the production of foodstuffs, crops, livestock, drinking water installations and supplies and irrigation works.

Article XV. Works or installations containing dangerous forces, namely dams, dykes and nuclear electrical generating stations, shall not be made the object of attack, even where these objects are military objectives, if such attack may cause the release of dangerous forces and consequent severe losses among the civilian population.

. . .

Appendix 3.7 Inhumane Weapon Convention [Geneva, 1980][8]

Depositary: United Nations Secretary-General. *Entry into force:* 1983. *States parties as of late 1989 include:* 28 of all *ca* 170 states (among them, China, France, and the USSR).

. . .

Protocol III, Article II.4. It is prohibited to make forests or other kinds of plant cover the object of attack by incendiary weapons except when such natural elements are used to cover, conceal or camouflage combatants or other military objectives, or are themselves military objectives.

. . .

References

Ferm, R. 1989. Major multilateral arms control agreements. *SIPRI Yearbook*, Oxford, 1989:475–504.

Goldblat, J. 1982. *Agreements for arms control: a critical survey*. London: Taylor & Francis, 387 pp.

Roberts, A., & Guelff, R. (eds). 1982. *Documents on the laws of war*. Oxford: Clarendon Press, 498 pp.

Schindler, D., & Toman, J. (eds). 1988. *Laws of armed conflicts: a collection of conventions, resolutions and other documents*. 3rd ed. Dordrecht, Netherlands: Martinus Nijhoff, 1033 pp.

[8]The Inhumane Weapon Convention was concluded in Geneva in 1980, and opened for signature in New York in 1981.

Appendix 4
Environmental Hazards of War in an Industrializing World: Relevant Multilateral Declarations (Excerpts)

Contents

Appendix 4.1 Declaration on the Human Environment [Stockholm, 1972]

Promulgator: United Nations Conference on the Human Environment, Stockholm, 5–16 June 1972 (UNGA, 1973). *Supporting states include:* 113 of all *ca* 170 states (among them, China, France, the United Kingdom, and the USA).

. . .

Principle XXI. States have . . . the responsibility to ensure that activities within their jurisdiction or control do not cause damage to the environment of other States or of areas beyond the limits of national jurisdiction.

. . .

Principle XXVI. Man and his environment must be spared the effects of nuclear weapons and all other means of mass destruction. States must strive to reach prompt agreement, in the relevant international organs, on the elimination and complete destruction of such weapons.

. . .

Appendix 4.2 World Charter for Nature [New York, 1982]

Promulgator: United Nations General Assembly (UNGA, 1982). *Supporting states include:* 112 of all *ca* 170 states (among them, China, France, the United Kingdom, and the USSR).

. . .

Article V. Nature shall be secured against degradation caused by warfare or other hostile activities.

. . .

Article XI.e. Areas degraded by human activities shall be rehabilitated for purposes in accord with their natural potential and compatible with the well-being of affected populations.

. . .

Article XII.b. Special precautions shall be taken to prevent discharge [into natural systems] of radioactive or toxic wastes.

. . .

Article XX. Military activities damaging to nature shall be avoided.

. . .

References

UNGA. 1973. *Report of the United Nations Conference on the Human Environment, Stockholm, 5–16 June 1972.* New York: UN General Assembly, Document No. A/CONF.48/14/Rev.1, 77 pp.

UNGA. 1982. *World Charter for Nature.* New York: UN General Assembly, Resolution No. 37/7 (28 Oct 82), 5 pp.

Index

Index compiled by Meg Davies (Society of Indexers)